Skyhorse Publishing books may be purchased in bulk at special discounts for sales promotion, corporate gifts, fund-raising, or educational purposes. Special editions can also be created to specifications. For details, contact the Special Sales Department, Skyhorse Publishing, 307 West 36th Street, 11th Floor, New York, NY 10018 or info@skyhorsepublishing.com.

Skyhorse and Skyhorse Publishing are registered trademarks of Skyhorse Publishing, Inc.®, a Delaware corporation.

Visit our website at www.skyhorsepublishing.com.

10 9 8 7 6 5 4 3 2 1

Library of Congress Cataloging-in-Publication Data is available on file.

Print ISBN: 978-1-5107-0522-7
Ebook ISBN: 978-1-5107-0523-4

Printed in China

CONTENTS

It's All About the Ribs

Pork ribs are the flagship of barbecue, a Titian masterpiece on steel grates, the *Citizen Kane* seasoned by smoke and by all accounts . . . delicioso! Every patio warrior has at least attempted to tenderize this unforgiving rack of enjoyment. From my experience working with novice grill technicians, the success rate for succulent ribs is about 50/50, and I'm being very generous.

Therefore, I present to you the most thorough education on preparing the best ribs ever seen in print. This monstrous tutorial is made possible by the long list of rib recipes on cable TV, selling its viewers empty promises of tender, juicy ribs. Similarly, the specifics of cooking pork spareribs has been underserved and shrouded around smoke (pun intended) in numerous cookbooks dedicated to the swine slabs. Lastly, the best cooking class doesn't always reveal all their secrets and the paying customers are often led to read between the lines.

Are you picking up what I'm putting down? Let's get started!

MY INSTRUMENTS

Here are my weapons of choice when I barbecue ribs from start to finish (minus the ingredients, which will be discussed ahead). They include what I use to prepare a fire, maintain the grill, prepare the meat, and cook to perfection:

Charcoal Grill

Charcoal Lump or Briquettes

Charcoal Chimney

Grill Brush

Ash Shovel

Silicone Baste Brush

Long Spatula and Tongs

Heat Resistant Gloves

Lighter

Newspaper/Charcoal Bag

Butcher Knife

Heavy-Duty Aluminum Foil

Paper Towels

Disposable Cutting Boards

Chunks of Smoke Wood

Barbecue Utility Table

Depending on what type of cooker you have, the list of items should vary a little. In addition, meat thermometers are optional; I don't tend to take the temperature of the ribs. Instead, I use techniques to feel and see when the ribs are done. More about that later.

RIB SELECTION

When pitmasters start talking ribs, it only implies *pork* ribs. Specifically, two cuts of pork ribs: spareribs and loin back ribs. Beef ribs or any other type of protein ribs are considered a regional delicacy. Even though ancillary ribs are tasty, only hog ribs are considered authentic.

Spareribs are rather fatty, meaty, and shaped irregularly. They are cut from the pork belly, which is commonly made into bacon. From the underside of the ribs, the bones are clearly visible on the slab. However, surrounding the bones is excess meat and cartilage. Most folks just trim this part off to make a clean, rectangular piece of meat. When this is done, the ribs are called St. Louis style. Pre-cut St. Louis style ribs are now commonly found in the meat section of your grocery store, but be prepared to pay more for something that only takes a couple of minutes to do yourself. Moreover, don't think about throwing away the trimmings because you can make them into a delicacy known to the barbecue community as *rib tips*.

Baby back ribs come from near the spine of the hog, where the loin (a lean cut of pork) is located. Typically, you may find the larger version, called loin back ribs, in a package at the grocery store, or you may be fortunate enough to find the baby backs in the meat case at your local meat market. Loin backs are meaty and are a leaner muscle compared to spareribs. As a result, they have less flavor, but they're still a good eat!

I recommend that you try a St. Louis style rack of ribs and a loin back rack of ribs to see which you like best. There are pro and cons for each. When I'm selecting ribs for competition, I'm going with whichever rack looks meatier, has more fat, has straight bones, and resembles close to a perfect rack of ribs. Also, don't be afraid to buy the vacuum-sealed ribs from club stores like Costco; they are excellent quality. Considering my ribs are being judged with prizes, and braggin' rights are at stake, I absolutely avoid meager ribs. Meager ribs are not worth the six hours of smoke paradise.

ADDITIONAL NOTES ABOUT RIBS . . .

Keep in mind that baby back ribs weigh less than two pounds—anything bigger than that are loin back ribs. In addition, spareribs are trimmed to make St. Louis style ribs. Thus, St. Louis style has nothing to do with how they are cooked.

Furthermore, loin backs ribs or St. Louis style ribs benefit most from the 3-2-1 method (which you will learn about).

TRIMMING/REMOVING MEMBRANE

Trimming is the initial step of the process in preparing ribs. When you buy pork ribs, they are not usually ready to cook immediately. There are a couple of things to look for to see if trimming is necessary. First, does it have a membrane? The membrane is a thin, but tough, white translucent film on the bone side of the rack of ribs. Rarely can you find ribs without the membrane. When you do find the membrane . . . ALWAYS REMOVE THE MEMBRANE.

If one is available, politely ask your butcher to remove the membrane for you. However, I suggest learning this technique yourself because it is an easy process to execute at home. For me, the best way to remove it is by prying up the edge of the membrane with a butter knife, against the last end rib bone. When enough of the membrane is pried off to pinch with your fingers, use a paper towel for gripping and remove the slimy membrane across the slab. It may take a few attempts to remove the whole membrane.

Once the membrane is removed, there are other trimming options for spareribs. But if these were loin back ribs (a.k.a. baby back ribs), nothing else would be left to trim. It is time to smoke 'em! Whole spareribs are an irregular mass of meat that was cut from the pork belly. In different regions of the country, spareribs are cooked whole. However, St. Louis style trimmed ribs are the preferred way to prepare barbecue ribs by most pitmasters. This style removes the cartilage surrounding the bones and shapes the ribs into a uniform size for even cooking.

To trim the whole spareribs into St. Louis style:
1. Lay the rack meat side down on a clean surface.
2. Locate the longest rib bone on the rack of ribs, which is how wide the rack of ribs will be.
3. So take your sharpened knife and make straight cuts perpendicular to each side of the longest rib bone.
4. Square up the ribs by cutting each end; the rack should be 18 to 24 inches in length.
5. Finally, cut off the flap on the bone side of the rack.
6. Save all those scraps you just trimmed away—those are your rib tips.

SEASONING RIBS

Flavoring ribs with sugars, herbs, and spices cannot be emphasized enough. Pork ribs already have great flavor because of the natural fat that is found between the bones and throughout the slab. But when combined with seasonings, the meat is enhanced and the surface develops a crust full of flavor. That exterior crust is commonly known as the bark. The bark is a prized condiment that adds complex flavors and textures. The casual barbecue connoisseur may see a burnt rack of ribs while the barbecue enthusiast sees a perfectly smoked slab. Ribs coated in a brown sugar–based rub and then smoked for hours display a sexy caramelization of sugars that showcases mahogany perfection. This is called the Maillard reaction (for all you foodie geeks)!

Each pitmaster has his or her own technique of seasoning ribs; consequently, some apply a heavy coat while others lightly dust. Even more hotly contested is the amount of time to let the meat rest after the rub has been applied! You may hear one person say that covering in plastic wrap overnight works best while another says to start cooking directly after the rub application. There is no wrong way to season ribs, just be sure to do it if you want ribs done right!

Since this is my show, sort of speak, I am more than happy to weigh in on this divisive subject. I like to season my ribs with a light coat of rub until it looks wet. Apply a second coat of rub and repeat with a third. For approximately 1 hour, let the ribs rest at room temperature so they can draw in the spices of the rub before cooking.

MARINADES, INJECTIONS, AND BRINES

To a lesser extent, liquid-based flavor enhancers serve as another layer of flavor and a means to retain moisture throughout the cooking process. While many pitmasters experiment with these techniques, the end product is met with mixed result. For example, brined ribs have the tendency to taste like ham and the marinades do not seem to penetrate the meat enough to infuse more flavor. Not all liquid methods will end up with these results; some folks swear by it and I am a believer.

BEST METHODS TO COOK RIBS

Arguably, barbecued ribs are deeply rooted in the fabric of American cuisine. Therefore, I consider slow smoked ribs to be the ideal method for this cut of meat. However, that does not mean other methods are inferior; on the contrary, they are meant to conveniently transform a tough cut of meat into one that can be enjoyed. Some methods are better than others from my experience, but if it works for you, go ahead and do it!

Indirect Heat: Ol' fashioned smoking. There is a reason that summer weekend warriors fire up their grill for ribs, to smoke 'em until they are tender. It's impossible to duplicate both the texture and aroma of a well smoked slab on anything inside the house. The only way to achieve this is applying indirect heat, which typically is offset or buffered by a heat shield or water pan over an open flame.

To those hard-core pitmasters that use only charcoal or wood, please avert your eyes from reading further, or skip to the next section:

For folks that use propane and natural gas grills, you can also benefit from the indirect heat method. By using the same approach as on a charcoal grill, cooking with gas can achieve the same tender and flavorful ribs. However, to say that this type of cooking can compete with smoke is like saying Salisbury steak tastes like a rib eye . . . please turn in your grill tech card.

AVOID

Parboiling: Purists pronounce, "sacrilege!" In the realm of cooking ribs, avoid boiling at all cost. Sure, heating ribs in a pot full of water will tenderize the meat, but all the flavor, texture, and appearance will be compromised. To hard-core BBQ snobs (like myself), it is not worth the degradation of such a costly cut of meat. With that said, it's all about personal preference . . . boil away if you wish.

Direct Heat: Will not work here because ribs have connective tissue that needs time to break down. By the time the ribs are hot enough to tenderize on the inside, the surface of the meat will be charred and tough.

BEST COOKING TEMPERATURE FOR RIBS

Connective tissue and cartilage woven into ribs make this an unforgiving cut of meat. Hours of exposure to low heat have long been the traditional way to cook ribs. Low and slow is still the standard, but somewhat higher temps are becoming chic for achieving sublime tenderness.

Low & Slow Smoking: 225–275°F. Picture a Saturday when Pop fires up the smoker, opens up a case of beer, and measures time with empty cans. You can't look at the clock when barbecuing; it's done when it's done. That's my kind of cooking and it's still widely considered "real" BBQ. We're doing our part to keep tradition alive.

Hot & Fast Smoking: 300–400°F. Need ribs in a pinch or done at a certain time? These temps are low enough to be considered BBQ and results have shown to be championship quality . . . literally! I have heard folks claim to cook perfectly tender ribs in about 90 minutes! Try it, you won't be disappointed.

Grilling: 450+°F. Ideal for roasting ribs, not BBQ. Temps these high are not unheard of and a well-known Memphis rib establishment made a name for themselves doing this. As a high heat critic, I have had excellent results cooking ribs at these temps.

COMPLEMENTARY WOOD FOR RIBS

When ribs are served at the local barbecue joint, focus is commonly on the dry rub and the sauce. What about the smoke? A decent rib shack knows a thing about its own product, so when a blank stare comes across the server's face when you ask about the smoke, cordially leave the grounds and never return. Smoke is essential for authentic ribs—it completes the trifecta of a full-flavored rack.

Choose your smoke wisely, or else risk overpowering your ribs. More subtle smoke such as fruit wood varieties—apple, cherry, and peach— are excellent for ribs. In the same regard, pecan and maple are pleasant as well. Notice I left out two traditionally dominant smoke woods, hickory and oak. Unless hickory or oak are found locally, pass on the stuff found in the retail chain stores. For example, if you live in Texas where post oak is bountiful, chances are you can find fresh smoke wood at your local meat market, fireplace store, landscape business, or neighbor. On the other hand, buying generic oak from your national depot hardware store would be risky because its low quality may negatively affect the flavor of your food. In addition, the smoke wood found in big box stores have suppliers that process wood covered with dirt, insects, and spiderwebs, and the wood is often kept under harsh conditions that may be suitable for a firepit but not for smoking your food.

RIB ACCESSORIES

As popular as ribs are to weekend warriors, few gadgets and gizmos exist for the salivating slab of pork. The most prominent accessory for ribs, and most replicated, is the rib rack. A rack can load multiple bands of ribs while saving valuable cooking space on the grill. Though it looks like nothing more than napkin holders attached together, the device is inexpensive and does its job for those with little room to lay ribs flat on the grates. Using one isn't difficult either; the slabs are slotted side by side while standing vertically. As a result, you can fit more ribs on the grill.

A lesser known accessory is a rotisserie rib cooking device. This version is not the typical rotisserie where you puncture the meat through a spit. Instead, a rib rotisserie has trays to lay the slabs flat while cooking. Furthermore, ribs are not the only meat you use on this gadget. Try chicken wings, hamburgers, potatoes, and sausages, too! Rotisserie cooking is a great way to produce flavorful ribs because the meat drippings baste the ribs as they rotate around and around.

OVERCOOKING VS. UNDERCOOKING

The most common error grill technicians make is not cooking the ribs long enough.

A popular misconception is that tough ribs are overcooked. Not true—tough ribs are due to undercooking the rack. Unlike other large cuts of meat like roasts, rounds, or tenderloins, ribs do not get tough at a higher internal cooking temp. On the contrary, due to its high concentration of connective tissue, fat, and collagen, ribs become tender with a higher internal temp.

DONENESS TESTS

There are several ways to check to make sure your smoked ribs are tender. Here are a few ways to tell:

The first indication is when the meat pulls back about ¼-inch from the bone (some pull back more than others).

Take a toothpick and poke between the bones at the thickest part of the ribs. If it easily slides in and out of the rack, it's done.

With a pair of tongs, grab one end of the ribs. If they bend easily, they are done. If not, keep them in the cooker.

No one test will determine whether the ribs are done; use the combination of all three. I promise that these tried-and-true techniques can help you achieve tender ribs bliss!

THE PERFECT BITE

A perfect bite is made up of three components: tenderness, moisture, and flavor. Tenderness for ribs is the delicate balance of not overcooking to the point of becoming mush. On the other hand, undercooking ribs render the slabs tough and chewy, like a two-dollar steak.

Ribs must be moist; this means that the juices can be seen in the meat. When the fat is properly rendered, it flavors and bastes the meat to juicy perfection. Nothing is more disappointing than dry or tough ribs.

A touch of sweetness complements this cut of meat best. Do not think that pouring honey all over ribs will make you grand champion; it won't. A combination of sweet, salty, tang, and heat must all be utilized to achieve a flawless balance of flavors.

Once you meet all the criteria above, having ribs with the perfect bite is easily achieved and something to be proud of.

3-2-1 SPARERIBS METHOD

What is 3-2-1?

3-2-1 represents the number of hours a rack of spareribs cooks at each stage. In other words, the ribs smoke for three hours, wrap for two hours, and cook without smoke for the last hour. Total, the ribs will spend six hours on the cooker. Do not use this technique on country ribs or beef ribs; they won't work as well because the country ribs are too lean and the cook times along with the flavor profile is all wrong for beef. Details of this are broken down even further as you continue to read.

The Plan

Basically, the 3-2-1 method calls for a simple list of ingredients that are applied at different steps in the process. This list of essentials includes:

Ribs

BBQ rub

Liquids (for foil wrap)

BBQ sauce

Canola oil

Sure, this list is short, but the ingredients themselves are complex and broad.

Step 1

If the ribs are frozen, thaw them out for approximately 3–4 days in the refrigerator. On the day of the cook, let the unfrozen ribs come to room temperature. While the ribs are sitting out, coat them with canola oil, then apply a sweet, sugar-based rub on the ribs by gently patting the rub into the meat. Let it sit until the rub turns into a syrup glaze.

During this time, prepare the cooker for smoking. You should have a smoker or a charcoal grill to cook ribs. If you have a charcoal grill, use the 2-zone method (cook in indirect heat until tender and then transfer to direct heat to caramelize). Set the temperature of the grill to approximately 225°F.

Note: I have done ribs on a gas grill and they turned out just fine.

Step 2

Wait about 20–30 minutes for the temperature to stabilize at 225°F . Add the glazed rack of ribs to the cooker, flesh side up. Remember, the lid is always on or closed with the vents wide open.

Add 2 or 3 chunks of dry seasoned hardwood/fruitwood to the smoker. Refer back to page 7.

Let the ribs smoke for 3 hours. Check the temperature often without opening the cooking chamber and keep it around 225°F. Also, check the charcoal and water/liquids as necessary.

Note: To achieve tender, moist ribs, make sure that there is a source for water in the cooking chamber. Humidity keeps the moisture inside the ribs. Typically, large trailer smokers create moisture by cooking large quantities of meat, but doing with one or two racks of ribs cannot produce moisture in the grill. So, adding a pan of water directly over the heat source or next to it can recreate that moisture.

Step 3

At 3 hours, the ribs could be considered ready to eat. But the connective tissue has not broken down at this point and the ribs would be tough and chewy. This next step will accelerate the breakdown of connective tissue, which will result in a tender product.

When the 3 hours are almost up, create a flat preparation area. Tear a sheet of aluminum foil, enough to completely wrap 1 rack of ribs. Remove the ribs from the grill and wrap the ribs in aluminum foil. Before you seal it up, add ¼ cup of apple juice. Doing this will expedite the cooking process of breaking down the meat and render off the fat. Seal it up tight so no liquids leak.

Note: Heavy-duty aluminum foil is recommended because the rib bones tend to puncture through cheaper foil, unless you double or triple wrap.

Place the ribs flesh side down on the grill grate and continue to cook at 225°F for 2 hours. Wood chunks are no longer needed, but continue to add water and charcoal.

Step 4

At 2 hours, remove the ribs from the smoker and unwrap the foil. They should look moist and the rub appear mealy. Notice how much the meat has pulled back from the bone. If there is about ¼ inch of bone showing, you're in good shape. If not, cook for another 30 minutes. Don't sweat it if the meat didn't pull back. The times are not a litmus test for doneness; you may have a thick rack of ribs that requires more time.

Keep the foil and all the juices inside of it. Shape the foil wrap into a boat with the ribs meat side up so that the ribs are exposed. Place the ribs back on the pit and apply more rub one last time. Cover with the lid and cook for the last hour to firm it up.

If you use barbecue sauce, now is the time to 1) take it out of the refrigerator to sit out at room temperature and 2) warm it up on the grill or stove. The popular application for barbecue sauce is to put it on 10 minutes before you take the ribs off the grill.

Step 5

Sauce the ribs in the final 10 minutes and check for doneness. Using the 3-2-1 method takes the guessing out of knowing when ribs are done. However, the 3-2-1 method typically does not produce fall-off-the-bone ribs for whole spareribs. To achieve fall-off-the-bone ribs, cook them longer in the foil wrap. This will further break down the meat. Do this with caution because eventually the meat will turn to mush and you can ruin a good rack of ribs. In other words, ribs are too expensive to make them fall off the bone. You can get the same results from pulled pork and it's cheaper!

If you want to apply this method to St. Louis style or loin back ribs, adjust by decreasing the cook times. Do this with a 2-2-1 or 3-1.5-.5 method to your desired tenderness.

FYI, if you didn't achieve a tender rack of ribs, cook them longer and keep checking for doneness (see page 8). Better results will only come with practice. No matter how perfect or imperfect they turned out to be, smoked ribs always taste good.

Step 6

Once the ribs are done, let them rest for a few minutes to cool off. When cutting the ribs, use a sharp, un-serrated knife. I cut mine into single or two bones so everybody can dig into those tender treats.

Congratulations, you successfully applied the 3-2-1 method! Enjoy those smoky meat sticks.

COMPETITION RIBS FLAVOR PROFILE

Competition Rub

Someone once told me approximately 90 percent of all BBQ competitors use commercial rubs. The reason being that there are a lot of quality rubs on the market and cooks have better things to do than play chef. Truth be told, I am a proponent of commercial rubs and there are many that claim to be championship quality.

Once in a while, I make my own rubs, but my homemade rubs are not quite as good as the rubs on the market. I find so many great BBQ rubs at the store that it's hard for me to stick with one. However, my favorite is Plowboys Yardbird rub. Many times I have started with the Yardbird rub and combined it with another rub with excellent results. But just for the record, I got first place using Plowboys alone. Listed below are more of my favorites:

Blues Hog
Dizzy Pig Pineapple
Penzey's BBQ 3000
Kosmo's Q Dirty Bird
Smokin' Guns Hot
Code 3 Spices 5-0

Using a combination of rubs is encouraged. Doing this is creating layers of flavors, which is critical in competition. Another trick I use is adding dark brown sugar on the ribs, which creates a beautiful mahogany bark. Brown sugar is actually the main ingredient in many pork-based rubs. The low temperature of the smoker or grill caramelizes the sugar and gives it an eye pleasing look and a delectable aroma.

COMPETITION FOIL WRAP

My competition ribs need this step in order to put mine over the top of everybody else's ribs. A special combination of rich ingredients go into my wrap. With these ingredients, I've taken third, second, and first place, so the judges obviously like the flavor profile.

Wrap ingredients:

Parkay margarine (squeeze "butter")

Turbinado sugar (Sugar in the Raw)

Honey

Tiger Sauce (sweet chile sauce)

This wrap recipe has been used by some of the best barbecue competition cooks in the world. What makes my award-winning ribs recipe different from everybody else's? Practice! More on using foil wraps on page 8.

COMPETITION SAUCE

I use a 50/50 mix of Blues Hog Original and Blues Hog Tennessee Red. I like to warm up the sauce to make it smooth and glossy. Then I apply it when the ribs are in the turn-in box, because I don't want my fingerprints showing and I want to cover up any undesirable blemishes.

The key to a great competition sauce is balancing flavors, with plenty of sweetness and just enough tang and heat to please the judges' taste buds. Finally, do not oversauce the ribs; use just enough to complement the meat, rubs, and smoke. Sauce is not required in competitions, but they will score higher than ones that don't have it. I haven't tried skipping the sauce myself, but what I'm doing seems to be working!

Cuts of Ribs

When you get to smoking meats as much as I do, you start to realize that one piece of meat can be cut in a slightly different way and given a new name, and it'll cost you $2 more a pound! I have come to embrace a lot of the less expensive cuts and most of the folks I serve them to absolutely love them.

So let's run through the Rolodex of common ways to prepare ribs. This way you can either save money and/or get mad street cred for knowing one cut from another.

Prep Tip:
In their raw state, ribs can be prepared whole or broken down to save time.

Pork Cuts
Whole Spareribs. The quintessential cut for all backyard barbecue enthusiasts. Whole spareribs contain the bones, cartilage, and flaps of meat sticking out in back of the ribs.

St. Louis Style Spareribs. This is the trimmed version of the whole spareribs. The cartilage and extra flaps of meat are removed, and what's left is a cleaner looking rack of ribs. The biggest misnomer is that St. Louis style ribs are a combination of St. Louis barbecue sauce and seasonings.

Rib Tips. The scraps that are trimmed off the whole spareribs to make St. Louis style spareribs are called rib tips. They are cooked as is or can be made into ground pork.

Baby Back Ribs. These come from the loin and near the spine of the hog. Typically, baby back ribs weigh less than two pounds. The larger back ribs (more than two pounds) are known as loin back ribs. *Country Ribs.* Huh? Those aren't ribs! That's right, they are not. But I grew up in California thinking that they were. They were boneless and delicious . . . so to me they will always be ribs.

Beef Cuts

Back Beef Ribs. Trimmed off the prime rib roast, these ribs have phenomenal flavor. However, the bones are huge and have very little meat.
Beef Short Ribs. The classic dinosaur ribs! One of these ribs is too much for one person to eat. Short ribs typically have six bones and a couple inches of meat sitting on top of the bones.
English. Beef short ribs that are cut into individual bones and cut again across the bone. They could be anywhere from half the length to only two inches long. These are popular for smoking because they take less time to cook and it's not a huge piece of meat on a stick.

Flanken. Another cut of beef short ribs that is thinly sliced, with the bone in. They're often used in Korean barbecue.

Presentation Tips:

When the ribs are cooked and ready to serve, these are some ways to kick up your presentation mojo.

Pork and Beef cuts

Whole Ribs. Release your inner Cro-Magnon and tear the meat from the bone. Nothing fancy about it, just go from smoker to plate here.
Individual Bones. Equally cutting the ribs into individual bones is the common serving preference. The classic meat lollipop!
Hollywood Cut. Seen in the barbecue competition world to give the judges more meat on a bone. One rib bone is cut wider by taking the meat from the neighboring bone, thus sacrificing two bones for one Hollywood rib.
Pulled Rib Meat. Repurpose leftover ribs by pulling the meat off the bone and using it as pulled pork.

Premium Cuts of Ribs

Being in the competition barbecue circuit brings a never-ending quest for finding ribs with more flavor. When the local grocery and warehouse store ribs become old hat for competition barbecue judges, hard-core barbecue enthusiast look for the most unique and best meat available.

Pork

There are two main options here, Berkshire and Duroc pork. These heritage breeds are bred to taste awesome! The amount of fat and the color of the meat lets you know that this is an exquisite piece of meat and it's going to melt in your mouth. Fortunately, these are not hard to find online. However, be prepared to pay extra because these are rare breeds.

Beef

Typically, most of us settle for a USDA Choice steak. It's what we have been given, from the meat market to our favorite steakhouse. It's time to treat yourself to the good stuff, USDA Prime. It's labeled with a gold sticker, so you know you got the real deal. Are you looking for even more flavor and boldness? Waygu beef is the ultimate in tenderness and flavor—you can't beat it. Waygu is harder to find than USDA Prime, but you can locate it online as well. Once again, be prepared to pay up!

Rib Philosophy

Everyone has an opinion about what you should do to make juicy, tender ribs. Occasionally, I get into a discussion about this guy's barbecued ribs being cooked in a slow cooker and how tender and flavorful they were. Is this barbecue blasphemy?

I don't believe so; if ribs in a slow cooker taste to him like the best thing ever, then so be it . . . that's how he should cook them. However, if you tell me that I should like slow cooker ribs better than smoked ribs, you're dead to me. I have my own style of smoking meat that I have been perfecting now for nearly ten years.

Here are common questions I get about my rib philosophy:

What is the best way to cook ribs?

Smoking ribs is the most authentic way to cook ribs and it so happens it is my favorite. I'm a traditional guy and using heat, smoke, and a grill doesn't get more authentic than that. At a distant second is frying pork ribs. Since I live in the Midwest, fried pork is common and available everywhere. And as if I needed more excuses to fry pork . . . Mexican cuisine has a couple of my favorite fried pork dishes, Milanese and Carnitas!

Which ribs have more flavor/better taste, baby back or spareribs?

Spareribs, without question. I realize that baby back ribs are more popular and easier to find at the grocery store or meat market; however, baby back ribs are cut from the loin. The pork loin isn't inherently flavorful—in fact, I highly recommend meat injections or a brine to add flavor to pork loin. As such with baby back ribs, they need flavor added.

On the other hand, pork spareribs are affixed to the pork belly of the hog. If you know a little bit about the culinary applications of pork belly, that's bacon. During processing, the pork belly is manually trimmed from the surface of the spareribs, so that is instant flavor!

What is the easiest and fastest way to cook barbecue ribs?

No matter what, I will never be convinced that ribs can be grilled over direct high heat and served tender. There isn't a short cut for cooking ribs if you want ribs that are tender and delicious. It takes time and patience, which is why most folks would rather go to a BBQ joint and spend $20 for what is a $9 slab of ribs at the meat market. Even if you're cooking ribs hot and fast, it's about a three-hour cook, which is still too long for most folks.

How do you make the rib meat fall off the bone?

Simple answer; overcook the meat. This is where having patience and cooking the ribs for a long period of time kicks in. All the connective tissue and fat strands need to melt before the rib meat pulls cleanly from the bone. If high heat (grilling) was applied here, at best you have burnt meat on the outside and raw or a cool internal temperature on the inside. It's important to have the temperature on the surface of the ribs be close to the internal temperature of the ribs. Maintain that temperature for hours and the meat will break free from the connective tissue and fat strands . . . and hence, fall off the bone.

CHAPTER 1

PORK SPARERIB RECIPES

APPLE HABANERO SPARERIBS

Serves: 4
Total time: 5 hours

Ingredients

1 rack pork spareribs, St. Louis style
Main Street Rib Rub (page 192)

Apple Habanero Glaze

1 cup apple jelly
2 habanero peppers, chopped
¼ cup hoisin sauce
1 tsp. apple cider vinegar
1 tsp. lime juice

Instructions

1. Set up the grill (or smoker) for indirect heat at 225°F. Use hickory, pecan, or any fruitwood for smoking.

2. Apply the rib rub evenly over the spareribs and place them on the grill.

3. Smoke for 3 hours.

4. In a saucepan on medium low heat, combine glaze ingredients and let simmer for an hour. Once the jelly has liquefied, use a stick blender to emulsify the sauce. Set sauce aside until ready to use.

5. Wrap the ribs in heavy-duty aluminum foil and place them back in the smoker, meat side up. Cook for 2 hours.

6. Unwrap the ribs and cook for 1 hour. Baste the ribs with the apple habanero glaze every 15 minutes.

7. Serve ribs immediately with a side of the glaze.

ATOMIC APPLE RIBS

Serves: 3
Total time: 5 hours

Ingredients

1 rack pork spareribs, St. Louis style
2 tbsp. canola oil
2 cups apple juice, in a spray bottle

Atomic Rub

2 tbsp. brown sugar
1 tbsp. Hungarian paprika
1 tsp. apple pie spice
½ tsp. garlic powder
½ tsp. onion powder
Black pepper
Kosher salt

Foil Wrap

2 cups brown sugar
1 cup apple jelly
½ cup Parkay squeeze margarine

Hot Cinnamon BBQ Sauce

¼ cup orange juice
½ cup Red Hots candy
1½ cups ketchup
3 tbsp. Worcestershire sauce
2 tbsp. molasses
2 tsp. Granny Smith apples, finely minced
1 tsp. garlic, finely minced
½ tsp. Hungarian paprika
¼ tsp. red pepper flakes

Instructions

1. Combine all Atomic Rub ingredients in a bowl and mix.

2. Set up smoker at 225°F. Add apple wood chunks for smoke.

3. Coat ribs with oil and apply the Atomic Rub. Let the rubbed ribs sit at room temperature until the rub becomes a syrup glaze, approximately 1 hour.

4. Smoke ribs on the smoker for 3 hours. Spray ribs with juice after the first hour and then in 30-minute intervals.

5. In the meantime, make the Hot Cinnamon BBQ Sauce. In a saucepan over medium heat, combine the orange juice and candy. Put the lid on and cook until the candy is melted down. Add remaining sauce ingredients into the saucepan, then mix well and reduce the heat to a simmer for 15 minutes. Sauce is done when thick. If not using the sauce immediately, let it cool and store it in a glass jar in the refrigerator.

6. Get 2 sheets of aluminum foil (enough to wrap the ribs) and place half of the wrap ingredients in the center. Place the ribs meat side down on the sugar-jelly-butter mix and top the ribs off with the other half of the ingredients. Wrap the ribs tightly in the foil and cook on the smoker for 2 hours.

7. Check for doneness and remove from the smoker. Unwrap the foil and turn the ribs meat side up. Rewrap in the foil and place back on the smoker for 1 hour to cook in their own juices.

8. In the last 10 minutes, apply Hot Cinnamon BBQ sauce.

9. Remove the ribs from the smoker and rest for 10 minutes. Slice into individual bones and serve immediately.

AUTHENTIC LOW AND SLOW SPARERIBS

Serves: 3
Total time: 6 hours

> No frills, no hype ribs. Make it all from scratch and be proud of the end results. This recipe is for sweet Kansas City style ribs, with a savory spice rub and a sticky, thick tomato-based sauce. You won't be disappointed.

Ingredients

1 rack pork spareribs, St. Louis style

¼ cup Main Street Rib Rub (page 192)

½ cup Hwy K Rib Sauce (page 193)

Instructions

1. Set up the grill (or smoker) for indirect heat at 225°F. Use hickory and/or peach wood.

2. Apply the rib rub evenly over the ribs and place them on the grill.

3. Smoke for 3 hours.

4. Wrap the ribs tight with heavy-duty aluminum foil. Place the ribs back on the smoker.

5. Cook for 2 hours.

6. Remove from the cooker, unwrap from aluminum foil, and cook for another hour. Brush with the Rib Sauce every 15 minutes.

7. Remove the ribs from the smoker and rest on a platter for 5 minutes. Slice the ribs into individual bones.

8. Serve immediately.

At the 2015 Wildwood BBQ Bash in St. Louis, MO. Over one hundred teams compete for trophies and bragging rights. My team has placed twice in the Top 10 for the ribs category, including an 8th place call in 2015.

BEER BATTERED SPARERIBS

Serves: 4
Total time: 4 hours

Ingredients

1 rack pork spareribs, St. Louis style
4 tbsp. Main Street Rib Rub (page 192)
2 cups self-rising flour
1 tbsp. paprika
1 egg
12 oz. Corona beer
Oil for deep frying

Instructions

1. Set up the grill (or smoker) for indirect heat at 225°F. Use hickory, pecan, or any fruitwood for smoking.

2. Apply 2 tablespoons of Rib Rub evenly over the pork ribs and place them on the grill.

3. Smoke for 3 hours.

4. Remove the ribs and let them rest until they are cool enough to handle.

5. In a large mixing bowl, combine 1 cup of flour, remaining 2 tablespoons Rib Rub, paprika, and the egg. Slowly whisk the beer in the bowl until all the ingredients are combined.

6. On a small plate, pour the rest of the flour and spread evenly. Slice the ribs into individual bones and coat each rib with flour. Discard what is left.

7. Fire up the deep fryer at 375°F. Coat the partially cooked ribs with flour and deep-fry them for 10 minutes or until they turn golden brown. Tip: Don't overcrowd the fryer; cook in small batches.

8. Serve ribs immediately.

BEST SPARERIBS

One of the best pitmasters not only in the St. Louis area, but in the country, Jeff Brinker has the magic touch for turning ribs into work of art. He's helped me develop my craft and taught me how to make my ribs POP! This recipe is an excellent example of that POP!

Serves: 12
Total time: 6 hours

Ingredients

3 racks pork spareribs, St. Louis style
1 cup yellow mustard
1 cup Italian dressing
1 cup Plowboys Yardbird BBQ Rub
2 cups Blues Hog Original BBQ Sauce
Pineapple juice, in a spray bottle

Foil Wrap

¾ cup brown sugar
¾ cup honey
6 tbsp. Parkay squeeze margarine
6 tbsp. pineapple juice

Instructions

1. One hour before cooking, mix mustard and Italian dressing together. Rub dressing mix into ribs.

2. Lightly coat each side of ribs with BBQ Rub.

3. Set up smoker for 275°F. Add apple wood for smoke.

4. Place the meat on the smoker, meat side up.

5. Close lid and smoke, maintaining 275°F.

6. Every ½ hour, mist with pineapple juice.

7. After 3 hours, double wrap each slab individually in foil. Place meat side down and add the brown sugar, honey, Parkay, and pineapple juice. Return to the pit.

8. After 1 more hour, open the foil and turn the ribs over so meat side is up. Lightly sprinkle with rub.

9. After 30 minutes, begin testing for doneness and start brushing Blues Hog sauce on meat side.

10. Let cool 10 minutes, and enjoy!

BIG GAME COCKTAIL PORK RIBS

Serves: 4
Total time: 6 hours

> Skip the wings, chips, dip, and nachos for the fooball championship game . . . getcha some RIBS! These spareribs are the perfect combination of sweet, savory, and spicy that will take your party game to the next level. Impress the benchwarmers with this recipe.

Ingredients

1 rack pork spareribs, St. Louis style

Base Rib Rub

2 tbsp. paprika
1 tsp. garlic salt
1 tsp. Lawry's Seasoned Salt
1 tsp. onion powder
½ tsp. ground black pepper
½ tsp. ground thyme, dried

Cocktail Sauce

½ cup grape jelly
½ cup Heinz Chili Sauce
1 tbsp. Worcestershire sauce
¼ cup maple syrup
2 tbsp. Frank's Red Hot Sauce

Instructions

1. Set up the grill (or smoker) for indirect heat at 225°F. Use hickory, pecan, or any fruitwood for smoking.

2. Combine all Base Rib Rub ingredients in a bowl and mix well. If not using immediately, store in a sealed container or storage bag until ready to use.

3. Apply the Rib Rub evenly on the ribs and place them on the grill. Smoke for 3 hours.

4. Wrap the ribs in heavy duty aluminum foil. Cook on the smoker for another 2 hours.

5. In a saucepan, cook jelly, chili sauce, Worcestershire sauce, syrup, and hot sauce on medium low heat for 1 hour. Set aside at room temperature until ready to use.

6. Unwrap ribs and brush on the Cocktail Sauce.

7. Place the ribs back on the smoker and cook for another hour. Baste the ribs every 15 minutes.

8. Slice the rack of ribs into individual bones.

9. Serve baby back ribs drizzled with Cocktail Sauce.

BLACKENED RIBS WITH SWEET CHILI GLAZE

Serves: 3
Total time: 6 hours

> This is my interpretation of southeast and Cajun flavors from vacation. Our annual family excursions in Sanibel Island, Florida, leave me salivating for the spicy yet sweet concoction of the Caribbean. I was curious to mix Southern flavor with Midwestern pork ribs . . . the results are phenomenal.

Ingredients

1 rack pork spareribs, St. Louis style

Blackening Rub

⅜ cup sweet paprika

¼ cup salt

2 tbsp. onion powder

2 tbsp. garlic powder

2 tbsp. cayenne pepper

1½ tbsp. white pepper

1½ tbsp. black pepper

1 tbsp. dried thyme

1 tbsp. dried oregano

½ cup sweet chili sauce

Instructions

1. Set up the smoker or grill for indirect cooking at 225°F.

2. Mix Blackening Rub ingredients together in a bowl.

3. Remove the membrane from the ribs and apply rub to the ribs, reserving 4 tablespoons of the rub for later.

4. Use cherry wood for smoke and place the ribs on the smoker.

5. Cook for 3 hours at 225°F.

6. Wrap the ribs tightly, meat side down, in heavy-duty foil.

7. Cook for another 2 hours in the foil.

8. Remove the ribs from the foil and discard the foil and its contents. Apply the reserved Blackening Rub on the ribs. Meanwhile, heat a large cast-iron skillet on medium-high. Sear the ribs on both sides until the rub turns black. Put the ribs back on the cooker.

9. Cook the ribs for another hour, meat side up, and apply a coat of sweet chili sauce (I suggest Maggi Thai Sweet Chili Sauce or Sun Zen Sweet Pepper Sauce) every 15 minutes.

10. Remove the ribs from the cooker, slice, and serve immediately.

BUFFALO RIBS

Serves: 3
Total time: 6 hours

> My next campaign is to tell folks to eat more ribs! Chicken is overrated. Not really, but be prepared to have your mind blown by these ribs. This was one of those moments when I asked myself, *Why didn't I think of that sooner?*

Ingredients

1 rack pork spareribs, St. Louis style
Main Street Rib Rub (page 192)

Foil Wrap

1 cup unsalted butter
1 cup Crystal Hot Sauce
2 tbsp. white vinegar

Blue Cheese Dipping Sauce

¼ cup mayonnaise
¼ cup sour cream
¼ cup blue cheese crumbles
1 tsp. white vinegar
1 tsp. lemon juice
Salt, to taste

Instructions

1. Set up the smoker or grill for indirect cooking at 225°F.
2. Remove the membrane from the ribs and apply 2 tbsp. of rub (or more/less to taste) on the ribs.
3. Use pecan wood for smoke and place the ribs on the smoker.
4. Cook for 3 hours at 225°F.
5. In a saucepan on medium-low heat, add Foil Wrap ingredients. Cook, stirring, until butter is melted.
6. In a bowl, combine all the Blue Cheese Dipping Sauce ingredients together and mix well. Refrigerate until ready to serve.
7. Wrap the ribs tightly in heavy-duty foil and add ½ the Foil Wrap mixture.
8. Cook for another 2 hours in the foil.
9. Remove the ribs from the foil and reserve the juices.
10. Cook for another hour or until tender.
11. Mix the other ½ of the Foil Wrap mixture and the reserved foil juice together and apply on ribs when they are done.
12. Serve with Blue Cheese Dipping Sauce.

CAPTIVA SUNSET RIBS

Serves: 3
Total time: 6 hours

Ingredients

1 rack pork spareribs, St. Louis style
Main Street Rib Rub (page 192)

Foil Wrap

¼ cup Key Lime and Mango BBQ sauce
1 tbsp. Main Street Rib Rub (page 192)

Key Lime and Mango BBQ Sauce

10.5 oz. key lime jelly
3 oz. tomato paste
½ cup white sugar
1 cup white vinegar
1 tbsp. onion powder
1 tbsp. mustard powder
1 tsp. garlic powder
2 tbsp. paprika
½ tsp. cayenne pepper
1 tsp. kosher salt
1 tsp. black pepper
1 cup finely chopped mango

Instructions

1. Set up the smoker or grill for indirect cooking at 225°F.

2. Remove the membrane from the ribs and apply 2 tbsp. of rub (or more/less to taste) to the ribs.

3. Use cherry wood for smoke and place the ribs on the smoker.

4. Cook for 3 hours.

5. Combine all the Key Lime and Mango BBQ Sauce ingredients (except mango) in a saucepan on medium heat and mix well. Cook for 15 minutes, and then use an immersion blender or food processor to blend smooth. Add the finely chopped mango and cook for another 5 minutes. Let the sauce cool at room temperature until ready to serve. Reserve ¼ cup for the foil wrap. Store in the refrigerator for up to 2 weeks.

6. After 3 hours, evenly coat the meat side of the ribs with the foil wrap ingredients.

7. Wrap the ribs tightly, meat side down, in heavy duty foil.

8. Cook for another 2 hours in the foil.

9. Remove the ribs from the foil and discard the foil and its contents.

10. Cook the ribs for another hour, meat side up, and apply a coat of BBQ sauce every 15 minutes.

11. Remove the ribs from the cooker and slice immediately. Serve ribs with more sauce.

CHERRY COLA RIBS

Serves: 3
Total time: 6 hours

> Sugary, sweet, cherry goodness plus swine equals insane flavor! If this isn't the definition of meat candy, I don't know what is.

Ingredients

1 rack pork spareribs, St. Louis style
Main Street Rib Rub (page 192)

Cherry Cola BBQ Sauce

½ liter cola
½ cup ketchup
1 cup brown sugar
½ cup apple cider vinegar
2 cups fresh cherries, pitted
2 tbsp. soy sauce
2 tbsp. maraschino cherry juice
½ tsp. red pepper flakes
1 tsp. chili powder
½ tsp. onion powder
½ tsp. garlic powder

Foil Wrap

¼ cup cola
1 tbsp. Main Street Rib Rub (page 192)

Instructions

1. Set up the smoker or grill for indirect cooking at 225°F.

2. Remove the membrane from the ribs and apply 2 tbsp. of rub (or more/less to taste) to the ribs.

3. Use cherry wood for smoke and place the ribs on the smoker.

4. Cook for 3 hours at 225°F.

5. In a saucepan on medium heat, reduce ½ liter of Pepsi for 1 hour or until it thickens into a syrup consistency.

6. Combine all the Cherry Cola BBQ Sauce ingredients in the saucepan and mix well. Cook for 15 minutes and then use an immersion blender or food processor to break up the cherries, but leave small chunks. Let the sauce cool at room temperature until ready to serve. Store in the refrigerator for up to 2 weeks.

7. Wrap the ribs tightly, meat side down, in heavy-duty foil, and add the Foil Wrap ingredients.

8. Cook for another 2 hours in the foil.

9. Remove the ribs from the foil, then discard the foil and its contents.

10. Cook the ribs for another hour, meat side up, and apply a coat of BBQ sauce every 15 minutes.

11. Remove the ribs from the cooker and slice immediately. Serve ribs with more sauce.

COLE'S SWEET HEAT RIBS

Cole is a great friend of mine who makes some of the best St. Louis style BBQ sauce. His sauces are thin, sweet, and tangy! He admitted that this rib recipe was one of his old competition recipes that he started using again . . . and won with it! Cole has another sauce called Sweet Velvet that will make any slab of ribs POP! Check out his website at www.colessweetheat.com.

Ingredients

1 rack pork spareribs, St. Louis style
2 tbsp. All Purpose Meat Rub (page 192)
Cole's Sweet Heat BBQ Sauce

Foil Wrap

1 stick unsalted butter
¼ cup brown sugar
¼ cup sriracha
⅛ cup light corn syrup

Instructions

1. Season the ribs with 2 tbsp. of rub (or more/less to taste).
2. Smoke the ribs at 250°F for 2 hours.
3. Wrap the ribs in foil with all the wrap ingredients for an hour.
4. Unwrap the foil and apply Cole's Sweet Heat BBQ Sauce.
5. Place the ribs back on smoker for ½ hour.
6. Slice into bones and serve immediately.

Notes:

1. Apply the 2-zone indirect heat setup if no smoker is available.
2. Use enough foil to wrap completely around the ribs. I recommend using 2 sheets for durability.
3. Add chunks of smoke wood such as apple, cherry, or peach.
4. Essentially, this applies a 2-1-1 method (see the 3-2-1 method on page 7).

COMPETITION RIBS

MULTI-TIME AWARD WINNING RECIPE

Serves: 6
Total time: 6 hours

> Ribs are the quintessential backyard torch bearer. Once you mastered these delicious meat sticks, you are designated awesome for life. My award winning ribs take an onslaught of sweet and tangy flavors to another level.

Ingredients

3 racks pork spareribs, St. Louis style
½ cup canola oil
4 cups apple juice, in a spray bottle
2 cups honey

Rubs

1 cup Kosmos Q Dirty Bird
1 cup Plowboys Yardbird
1 cup turbinado sugar

Foil Wrap

1 cup Parkay squeeze margarine
12 cups dark brown sugar
½ cup Tiger Sauce

Sauce

4 cups Blues Hog Original, warm

Instructions

1. Apply a light coat of canola oil on all the ribs. Apply the rubs and turbinado sugar evenly on each rack and let ribs sit at room temperature to develop glaze (an hour).

2. Set up smoker at 250°F.

3. Place ribs on grill and add cherry wood to the fire to develop the smoke ring.

4. Spray apple juice after the first hour, then every 20 minutes after. Check ribs at 2 hours; smoke no longer than 3 hours.

5. Prepare 3 foil wraps: tear off 2 sheets of foil for each rack of ribs, making sure they're long enough to wrap the ribs completely.

6. In the center of the foil wrap, combine the Foil Wrap ingredients, reserving a little. Place the ribs meat side down on the ingredients. Apply reserved wrap ingredients to the bone side of the ribs.

7. Wrap tight with 2 sheets and cook for up to 2 hours, checking ribs after 1 hour.

8. When the ribs are tender, unwrap foil. Apply Yardbird rub on bone side.

9. Turn meat side up and apply Yardbird rub, then squeeze honey over ribs.

10. Cook for ½ hour in the foil juices. Spray juice every 10 minutes to keep surface moist.

11. Remove from cooker after 30 minutes. Allow ribs to rest on unwrapped foil for 10 minutes or until cool enough to handle. Slice immediately.

12. Place ribs meat side up on a cutting board. Brush sauce evenly over ribs.

13. Use a sharp knife to slice between ribs. Place ribs in a foil-lined pan and apply more honey.

14. Brush warm BBQ sauce on the ribs and serve.

DELTA PORK SPARERIBS

Serves: 2
Total time: 6 hours

Ingredients
1 rack pork spareribs, St. Louis style

Creole Spice Rub
½ cup paprika
1 tbsp. onion powder
1 tbsp. garlic powder
1 tbsp. cumin
½ tbsp. thyme
½ tbsp. cayenne pepper
1 tbsp. Old Bay Seasoning
1 tsp. ground allspice
1 tsp. white pepper
1 tsp. black pepper
1 tsp. kosher salt

Foil Wrap
1 cup Worcestershire sauce
½ cup Louisiana Hot Sauce
½ cup pineapple juice

Sauce
½ cup Hwy K Rib Sauce (page 193)

Instructions

1. Fire up the grill for indirect heat (or use a smoker), set at 225°F. Use hickory, pecan, or any fruitwood for smoking.

2. In a bowl, combine all the Creole Spice Rub ingredients and mix well.

3. Generously apply the spice rub on both sides of the ribs. When the rub turns into a glaze, place the ribs in the smoker.

4. Using the 3-2-1 method (see page 7), smoke the ribs for 3 hours.

5. Tear off a sheet of heavy-duty aluminum foil to wrap the ribs. In the center of the foil, add the Foil Wrap ingredients.

6. Place the ribs meat side down on the foil and wrap tightly. (Wrap with another sheet of foil to avoid tearing.)

7. Cook for 2 hours.

8. Unwrap the ribs (reserve ¼ cup of wrap liquid) and place ribs back on the smoker for 1 hour.

9. Combine Hwy K Rib Sauce and wrap liquid, mix well, and use it to baste the ribs every 15 minutes.

10. Slice ribs, baste with sauce, and serve immediately.

GARLIC HERB RUBBED PORK RIBS

Serves: 2
Total time: 6 hours

Ingredients

1 rack pork spareribs, St. Louis style

Garlic Herb Rub

3 tbsp. garlic salt

1 tsp. chili powder

1 pk. Goya Sazón (optional)

1 tbsp. onion powder

1 tsp. paprika

½ tsp. tumeric

1 tsp. ground thyme

1 tsp. dried parsley

Instructions

1. In a bowl, combine all Garlic Herb Rub ingredients and mix well. If not using immediately, store in an airtight container or a storage bag until ready to use.

2. Set up the grill (or smoker) for indirect heat at 225°F. Use hickory, pecan, or any fruitwood for smoking.

3. Apply the herb rub evenly over spareribs and place them on the grill.

4. Smoke for 3 hours.

5. Wrap the rack of ribs in heavy-duty aluminum foil and cook for 2 hours.

6. Unwrap the ribs and place the rack back on the cooker for 1 hour.

7. Remove the ribs from the cooker and rest for 10 minutes or until it is cool enough to handle.

8. Slice the rack into individual bones and serve immediately.

HIGH HEAT SPARERIBS

Serves: 2
Total time: 3 hours

The world of barbecue is a subculture of belief and trends. The hot and fast style of cooking barbecue has been around since barbecue itself. However, the application of using high heat to smoke ribs (and other meats) has been a hot trend recently in competition barbecue. And the results are proof among the believers. For example, the most recent winners of the American Royal and World Food Championships used the hot and fast method. Are you a believer?

Ingredients

1 rack pork spareribs, St. Louis style
¼ cup Main Street Rib Rub (page 192)
½ cup Hwy K Rib Sauce (page 193)

Foil Wrap

2 tbsp. unsalted butter
1 cup brown sugar
½ cup sweet chili sauce

Instructions

1. Set up the grill (or smoker) for indirect heat at 350°F. Use hickory and/or peach wood.

2. Apply the Main Street Rib Rub evenly over the ribs and place them on the grill.

3. Smoke for 1 hour.

4. Wrap the Foil Wrap ingredients and ribs tightly with heavy-duty aluminum foil. Place the ribs back on the smoker. Cook for 1½ hours.

5. Remove from the cooker, unwrap from aluminum foil, and cook for another 30 minutes. In the last 10 minutes of cooking, brush with the wrap glaze.

6. Remove the ribs from the smoker and rest on a platter for 5 minutes. Brush more glaze over the ribs and slice the ribs into individual bones.

7. Serve immediately.

My home state of Missouri, the Show Me State, is the leading producer of charcoal. At one time, Missouri produced 90 percent of charcoal for all barbecue enthusiasts.

IPA MUSTARD BBQ RIBS

Serves: 2
Total time: 6 hours

Ingredients

1 rack pork spareribs, St. Louis style
2 tbsp. Main Street Rib Rub (page 192)

IPA Mustard Sauce

⅓ cup yellow mustard
¼ cup IPA Beer (or any hoppy type of beer)
¼ cup white sugar
3 tbsp. honey
3 tbsp. ketchup
2 tbsp. white vinegar
2 tbsp. Frank's Hot Sauce
2 tbsp. whole grain mustard
2 tbsp. Dijon mustard
1 tbsp. Worcestershire sauce
1 tsp. liquid smoke
1 tsp. black pepper

Instructions

1. In a saucepan on medium-low heat, combine IPA Mustard Sauce ingredients and let simmer for an hour.

2. Set sauce aside at room temperature until ready to use.

3. Set up the grill (or smoker) for indirect heat at 225°F. Use hickory, pecan, or any fruitwood for smoking.

4. Apply the Main Street Rib Rub evenly over the spareribs and place them on the grill. Smoke for 3 hours.

5. Wrap the ribs in heavy-duty aluminum foil and place them back in the smoker, meat side up. Cook for 2 hours.

6. Unwrap the ribs and cook for 1 hour. Baste the ribs with the mustard sauce every 15 minutes.

7. Serve ribs immediately with IPA Mustard Sauce drizzled over the ribs.

JEFF'S ST. LOUIS STYLE RIBS

Jeff Fitter has been to a couple of the most prestigious BBQ contests on the circuit such as the Houston Livestock Show and Rodeo BBQ Championships and Murphysboro, Illinois, for the Apple City barbecue competition. When Jeff competes as Phatso's BBQ team, he takes his rib game up a notch with this recipe. Check out his site at www.phatsosbbq.com.

Serves: 9
Total time: 5 hours

Ingredients

3 racks pork spareribs, St. Louis style
½ cup Hwy K Rib Sauce (optional) (page 193)

Jeff's St. Louis Style Rub

1 cup brown sugar
1 cup white sugar
⅓ cup celery salt
⅓ cup black pepper
⅓ cup garlic powder
⅓ cup dry mustard
⅓ cup onion powder
1 tbsp. cayenne pepper

Instructions

1. Mix Jeff's St. Louis Style Rub ingredients together in a bowl and then set aside.

2. Trim the ribs by removing any large chunks of meat and, if needed (due to space limits or just because they look bad), remove the last few ribs on either end of the rack. You can cook them separately; we call them "tidbits!"

3. Start applying the rub on the back side of the ribs, just enough to see it's there. The back side needs flavor, too! Now flip the rib over and apply the rub to the meat side, covering it completely.

4. Repeat above until all ribs are rubbed. Then leave on tray or wrap and store in refrigerator or cooler for 3–12 hours to let that flavor settle in.

5. Bring smoker up to 250°F and have your smoking wood ready—cherry wood, pecan wood, or both.

6. Place the ribs on the smoker and close the lid (or door). Remember if you're looking, they ain't cooking!

7. Cook for about 4 hours, though time may vary depending on the smoker used. To determine when the rib is ready to serve, use a set of tongs to pick the rack up from the middle. The rib should bend until it makes a sort of frown; you will see the meat pulling but not tearing apart. If the ribs don't bend that much, cook for another 30 minutes and test again. Repeat until the ribs pass the bend test.

8. If desired, add your favorite BBQ sauce.

JERK RIBS

Serves: 2
Total time: 6 hours

Ingredients

1 rack pork spareribs, St. Louis style
Allspice berries
Cinnamon sticks

Jerk Marinade

8 habenero peppers, deveined and deseeded
6 jalapeño peppers, deveined and deseeded
¼ cup orange juice
2 tbsp. ground allspice
3 sprigs thyme, chopped
8 stalks green onion, chopped
1 tsp. ground nutmeg
1 tsp. ground cinnamon
¼ cup white sugar
2 tbsp. blackstrap molasses
2 tbsp. extra virgin olive oil
½ cup white vinegar
2 tbsp. kosher salt
1 tbsp. ground black pepper

Instructions

1. Make the Jerk Marinade at least a day or two before making the ribs, so the flavors have time to blend. Combine all Jerk Marinade ingredients in a food processor or blender, working in small batches if needed. Blend until mixed well and there are no large chunks; you want the consistency of pesto sauce. Store in the refrigerator for up to 1 month.

2. When ready to make the ribs, pour Jerk Marinade into a 2.5 gallon storage bag.

3. Remove the membrane from the ribs.

4. Place the ribs in the storage bag, seal it, and marinate in the refrigerator at least 2 hours and up to 24 hours.

5. Remove ribs from marinade. *Do not wipe off marinade.*

6. Set up the smoker or grill for indirect cooking at 225°F.

7. Use pecan wood, allspice berries, and cinnamon sticks for smoke. Place the ribs on the smoker.

8. Cook for 3 hours, meat side up, at 225°F.

9. Wrap the ribs tightly, meat side down, in heavy-duty aluminum foil.

10. Cook for another 2 hours in the foil.

11. Remove the ribs from the foil, discarding the foil and its contents.

12. Cook the ribs for another hour, meat side up, until tender.

13. Remove the ribs from the cooker, slice, and serve ribs immediately.

KING GARLIC RUBBED SPRARERIBS

Serves: 2
Total time: 6 hours

Ingredients

1 rack pork spareribs, St. Louis style

King Garlic Rib Rub

3 tbsp. dried garlic flakes

3 tbsp. dried red bell peppers

2 tbsp. white sugar

2 tbsp. dried roasted garlic flakes

1 tsp. crushed red pepper

1 tsp. garlic salt

1 tsp. turmeric

1 tsp. paprika

Instructions

1. Combine all King Garlic Rib Rub ingredients in a bowl and mix well.

2. Store in an airtight container or a storage bag until ready to use.

3. Set up the grill (or smoker) for indirect heat at 225°F. Use hickory, pecan, or any fruitwood for smoking.

4. Apply the King Garlic Rib Rub evenly over spareribs and place it on the grill. Smoke for 3 hours.

5. Wrap the rack of ribs in heavy-duty aluminum foil. Cook for 2 hours.

6. Unwrap the ribs and place the rack back on the cooker for 1 hour.

7. Remove the ribs from the cooker and rest for 10 minutes or until cool enough to handle.

8. Slice the rack into individual bones and serve immediately.

I became head pitmaster of Fireside Smokers BBQ Team in 2014. We compete in and around the St. Louis area as a member of the St. Louis Barbecue Society.

MEMPHIS DRY RUBBED RIBS

Serves: 2
Total time: 6 hours

Ingredients

1 rack pork spareribs, St. Louis style

Memphis Dry Rub

¼ cup paprika

3 tbsp. garlic salt

2 tbsp. chili powder

2 tbsp. brown sugar

2 tbsp. dried oregano

1 tbsp. dried thyme

1 tbsp. dried onion flakes

1 tbsp. red pepper flakes

½ tbsp. dried basil

½ tsp. ground cinnamon

½ tsp. ground nutmeg

1 tbsp. seasoned salt

1 tsp. black pepper

Instructions

1. Combine all Memphis Dry Rub ingredients in a bowl and mix well. Store in an airtight container or a storage bag until ready to use.

2. Set up the grill (or smoker) for indirect heat at 225°F. Use hickory, pecan, or any fruitwood for smoking.

3. Apply the Memphis Dry Rub evenly over spareribs and place it on the grill. Smoke for 3 hours.

4. Wrap the rack of ribs in heavy-duty aluminum foil. Cook for 2 hours.

5. Unwrap the ribs and place the rack back on the cooker for 1 hour.

6. Remove the ribs from the cooker and rest for 10 minutes or until cool enough to handle.

7. Slice the rack into individual bones, season with more rub, and serve immediately.

MEXICAN ADOBO SPARERIBS

Serves: 2
Total time: 6 hours

Ingredients
1 rack pork spareribs, St. Louis style

Mexican Adobo Rub
4 tbsp. lemon pepper
3 tbsp. garlic salt
1 tsp. turmeric
1 pk. Goya Sazón
1 tsp. cumin
1 tbsp. onion powder

Instructions
1. Combine all Mexican Adobo Rub ingredients in a bowl and mix well. Store in an airtight container or a storage bag until ready to use.

2. Set up the grill (or smoker) for indirect heat at 225°F. Use hickory, pecan, or any fruitwood for smoking.

3. Apply the rub evenly over spareribs and place it on the grill. Smoke for 3 hours.

4. Wrap the rack of ribs in heavy-duty aluminum foil. Cook for 2 hours.

5. Unwrap the ribs and place the rack back on the cooker for 1 hour.

6. Remove the ribs from the cooker and rest for 10 minutes or until they are cool enough to handle.

7. Slice the rack into individual bones and serve immediately.

MOJO RIBS

(pronounced MO-HO)

Serves: 2
Total time: 6 hours

Ingredients

1 rack pork spareribs, St. Louis style
Latin hot sauce (Valentina Extra Hot or your favorite type)

Mojo Marinade

2 cups sour orange juice
¼ cup olive oil
1 large yellow onion, sliced thin
2 tbsp. minced garlic
2 tbsp. red wine vinegar
2 tsp. cumin
1 tsp. Mexican oregano
Salt and pepper, to taste
¼ cup fresh cilantro

Citrus Rub

4 tbsp. chili powder
2 tbsp. lemon pepper
2 tsp. garlic salt

Foil Wrap

¼ cup olive oil
1 tbsp. Citrus Rub

Instructions

1. In a 2.5 gallon storage bag, combine all marinade ingredients and mix well.

2. Remove the membrane from the ribs.

3. Place the ribs in the storage bag, seal it, and marinate in the refrigerator at least 2 hours and up to 24 hours.

4. Remove ribs from marinade and wipe off any excess debris. Discard the marinade and keep the ribs at room temperature for 1 hour before cooking.

5. Set up the smoker or grill for indirect cooking at 225°F.

6. Mix Citrus Rub ingredients together in a bowl and apply to the ribs.

7. Use oak wood for smoke and place the ribs on the smoker.

8. Cook for 3 hours, meat side up, at 225°F.

9. In a small bowl, combine Foil Wrap ingredients and mix well. Leave at room temperature until ready to use.

10. Evenly coat the meat side of the ribs with the Foil Wrap mixture. Wrap the ribs tightly, meat side down, in heavy-duty foil.

11. Cook for another 2 hours in the foil.

12. Remove the ribs from the foil, discarding the foil and its contents.

13. Cook the ribs for another hour, meat side up, until tender.

14. Remove the ribs from the cooker and serve ribs immediately with your favorite hot sauce. I prefer Valentina Extra Hot.

NAPA VALLEY RIBS

Serves: 2
Total time: 6 hours

Ingredients

1 rack pork spareribs, St. Louis style
2 tbsp. Main Street Rib Rub (page 192)
½ cup Hwy K BBQ Rib Sauce (page 193)

Foil Wrap

¼ cup turbinado sugar
¼ cup hot pepper jelly
¼ cup squeezable margarine
¼ cup Napa red wine

Instructions

1. Set up grill for indirect cooking at 250°F.

2. Remove membrane from the ribs and apply Main Street Rib Rub to the ribs.

3. Use apple wood for smoke and place the ribs on grill.

4. Cook for 3 hours at 250°F.

5. Then wrap ribs tightly in heavy-duty foil and add the Foil Wrap ingredients.

6. Cook for another 2 hours in the foil.

7. Next, remove the foil, but reserve the juices.

8. Cook for another hour or until tender.

9. Mix 50/50 of warm rib sauce and the foil juice reserve together and apply to ribs when they are done.

O'FALLON SEASONED PORK RIBS

Serves: 2
Total time: 6 hours

Ingredients

1 rack pork spareribs, St. Louis style

O'Fallon Rib Rub

3 tbsp. garlic salt
2 tbsp. brown sugar
1 tsp. chili powder
1 pk. Goya Sazón (optional)
1 tbsp. onion powder
1 tbsp. dried red bell peppers
1 tsp. paprika
1 tsp. dried parsley

Instructions

1. In a bowl, combine all O'Fallon Rib Rub ingredients and mix well.

2. Store in an airtight container or a storage bag until ready to use.

3. Set up the grill (or smoker) for indirect heat at 225°F. Use hickory, pecan, or any fruitwood for smoking.

4. Apply the O'Fallon Rib Rub evenly over spareribs and place ribs on the grill. Smoke for 3 hours.

5. Wrap the rack of ribs in heavy-duty aluminum foil. Cook for 2 hours.

6. Unwrap the ribs and place the rack back on the cooker for 1 hour.

7. Remove the ribs from the cooker and allow to rest for 10 minutes or until they are cool enough to handle.

8. Slice the rack into individual bones and serve immediately.

PACIFIC SPARERIBS

Serves: 2
Total time: 6 hours

Ingredients
1 rack pork spareribs, St. Louis style

Pacific Rib Rub
2 tbsp. paprika
2 tbsp. brown sugar
2 tsp. Chinese five-spice powder
1 tbsp. garlic salt
1 tbsp. onion powder
1 tsp. cayenne pepper

Foil Wrap
1 star anise, whole
½ cup brown sugar
¼ cup soy sauce
¼ cup pineapple juice
2 whole bay leaves, dried
3 tbsp. red wine vinegar
2 tsp. onion powder
2 tsp. garlic powder

Instructions
1. Combine all Pacific Rib Rub ingredients in a bowl and mix well. Store in an airtight container or a storage bag until ready to use.

2. Set up the grill (or smoker) for indirect heat at 225°F. Use hickory, pecan, or any fruitwood for smoking.

3. Apply the rib rub evenly over the pork ribs and place them on the grill. Smoke for 3 hours.

4. In a saucepan on medium-low heat, add all the Foil Wrap ingredients and cook down for 1 hour.

5. Wrap ribs and Foil Wrap ingredients in heavy-duty aluminum foil. Cook for 2 hours.

6. Unwrap the ribs and cook for 1 hour on the smoker. Do not discard the glaze in the foil wrap. Use the glaze to baste the ribs every 10 minutes.

7. Remove the rack of ribs from the smoker and allow to rest until it is cool enough to handle.

8. Slice ribs into individual bones and serve immediately with the glaze drizzled on top.

PIG CRUSTED PORK RIBS

Serves: 2
Total time: 6 hours

Ingredients

1 rack pork spareribs, St. Louis style
½ lb. bacon, cooked and chopped
¼ lb. pork rinds, crushed
Main Street Rib Rub (page 192)

Instructions

1. Set up smoker (or grill) for indirect heat at 225°F. Use hickory, pecan, or any fruitwood for smoke in this recipe.

2. Apply Main Street Rib Rub evenly over the ribs.

3. Smoke ribs for 3 hours.

4. Wrap ribs tightly in heavy-duty aluminum foil and cook for 2 hours.

5. Unwrap the ribs, discard foil, and cook for 1 hour.

6. Smash the bacon crumbles/crushed pork rinds on top of the ribs.

7. Slice and serve.

RANCHERO PORK RIBS

Serves: 2
Total time: 6 hours

Ingredients

1 rack pork spareribs, St. Louis style
⅓ cup shredded Oaxaca cheese
2 cups shredded lettuce
¼ cup roasted corn kernels
1 Roma tomato, diced
¼ cup sour cream
3 tbsp. Valentina's Hot Sauce
1 tbsp. lime juice
¼ cup Cotija cheese

Ranchero Rub

3 tbsp. chili powder
1 tsp. ground cumin
1 tsp. brown sugar
1 tsp. paprika
½ tsp. onion powder
½ tsp. garlic salt
½ tsp. coriander
½ tsp. ground cinnamon

Instructions

1. Combine all Ranchero Rub ingredients in a bowl and mix well. Store in an airtight container or storage bag until ready to use.

2. Set up the grill (or smoker) for indirect heat at 225°F. Use hickory, pecan, or any fruitwood for smoking.

3. Apply the Ranchero Rub evenly over the spareribs and place them on the grill. Smoke for 3 hours.

4. Wrap the ribs tightly in heavy-duty aluminum foil. Place back on the cooker for 2 more hours.

5. Unwrap the ribs and cook 1 hour.

6. Place the ribs on a serving platter and cover them with the Oaxaca cheese. Slice the ribs into individual bones and top the ribs with the lettuce, corn, and tomato.

7. In a bowl, combine the sour cream, hot sauce, and lime juice, and mix well. Pour the creamy hot sauce over the ribs and top with Cotija cheese.

8. Serve immediately.

Fundraisers and charity events around St. Louis will most certainly involve the sale of barbecue ribs. Folks reciprocate the tradition and buy racks of pork ribs for a great cause.

ROTISSERIE SEASONED PORK RIBS

Serves: 2
Total time: 6 hours

Ingredients

1 rack pork spareribs, St. Louis style

Rotisserie Rub

3 tbsp. seasoned salt
1 tbsp. onion powder
1 tbsp. garlic powder
1 tsp. chili powder
1 tsp. paprika
1 tsp. dried parsley

Instructions

1. Combine all Rotisserie Rub ingredients in a bowl and mix well.

2. Store in an airtight container or a storage bag until ready to use.

3. Set up the grill (or smoker) for indirect heat at 225°F. Use hickory, pecan, or any fruitwood for smoking.

4. Apply the Rotisserie Rub evenly over spareribs and place them on the grill. Smoke for 3 hours.

5. Wrap the rack of ribs in heavy-duty aluminum foil. Cook for 2 hours.

6. Unwrap the ribs and place the rack back on the cooker for 1 hour.

7. Remove the ribs from the cooker and allow to rest for 10 minutes or until they are cool enough to handle.

8. Slice the rack into individual bones and serve immediately.

SOUTH CAROLINA RIBS YANKEE STYLE

This is an award-winning recipe from Steven Marx of Tell You What BBQ. Check out his site at www.tellyouwhatbbq.com.

Serves: 6
Total time: 6 hours + marinating

Ingredients

3 racks pork spareribs, St. Louis style
¼ cup yellow mustard
½ cup Dizzy Pig Dizzy Dust Rub
½ cup Dizzy Pig Swamp Venom Rub
1 cup light brown sugar
4 cups apple cider, in a spray bottle

South Carolina Mustard Sauce

½ cup yellow mustard
¼ cup apple cider vinegar
5 tbsp. dark brown sugar
½ tsp. paprika
½ tsp. Worcestershire sauce
½ tsp. white pepper
½ tsp. cayenne pepper
¼ tsp. black pepper

Instructions

1. Combine all South Carolina Mustard Sauce ingredients in a medium saucepan over medium heat.

2. Stir until all ingredients are dissolved and mixed well. Allow to cool.

3. Remove membrane from ribs and trim large fat deposits.

4. Coat ribs with mustard. Mix dry rubs together and apply about half to the ribs. Light coating is key for this step. Wrap ribs in aluminum foil and refrigerate overnight.

5. Unwrap ribs and place on smoker for 2 hours at 250°F.

6. Remove ribs from smoker and coat liberally with brown sugar. Re-rub ribs with remaining dry rub mix. Return to smoker for 2 more hours, spritzing with apple cider every half hour.

7. At hour 4, begin to baste ribs with South Carolina Mustard Sauce. Baste liberally (dripping) at 4 hours and 4½ hours.

8. Remove ribs after 5 to 5½ hours and wrap in heavy-duty aluminum foil. Allow to rest for a half hour before cutting. Turn ribs upside down to cut. Apply final sauce polish in the turn-in box.

My rib cooker is a Yoder YS640. It's a pellet cooker, and I love it! All it does is win!

SOUTHERN SMOKED PORK RIBS WITH VINEGAR SAUCE

Serves: 4
Total time: 6 hours

It doesn't get simpler or more authentic than this in the backyard. This is the type of cooking that takes place on a weekend during the summer, napping in your zero gravity chair partially covered by the shade . . . but too lazy to move completely into the shade. You'll know when the ribs are done by how many ice cold beers you drank.

Ingredients

1 rack whole spareribs, untrimmed

Southern Rib Rub

3 tbsp. coarse black pepper

3 tbsp. kosher salt

1 tsp. cayenne pepper

Vinegar Sauce

⅓ cup Hwy K Rib Sauce (page 193)

2 tbsp. yellow mustard

⅓ cup apple cider vinegar

¼ cup white vinegar

¼ cup honey

1 tbsp. black pepper

1 tbsp. red pepper flakes

Instructions

1. Combine all Southern Rib Rub ingredients in a bowl and set aside until ready to use.

2. In a saucepan on low heat, combine all Vinegar Sauce ingredients and mix well.

3. Cook for 30 minutes and stir often.

4. Turn off heat and set aside until ready to use.

5. Set up the grill (or smoker) for indirect heat at 225°F. Use hickory and/or peach wood.

6. Apply the Southern Rib Rub evenly over the ribs and place them on the grill. Smoke for 3 hours.

7. Wrap the ribs tightly with heavy-duty aluminum foil. Place the ribs back on the smoker. Cook for 2½ hours.

8. Remove from the cooker, unwrap from aluminum foil, and cook for another hour. Baste with the vinegar sauce every 15 minutes.

9. Remove the ribs from the smoker and rest on a platter for 10 minutes. Slice the ribs into individual bones. Baste ribs with more vinegar sauce.

10. Serve immediately.

SPARERIBS WITH ASIAN PEACH GLAZE

Serves: 4
Total time: 5 hours

Ingredients

1 rack pork spareribs, St. Louis style
Main Street Rib Rub (page 192)

Asian Peach Glaze

½ cup peach preserves
¼ cup Thai sweet chili sauce
1 tbsp. sriracha sauce
1 tbsp. lime juice
½ tbsp. chopped cilantro

Instructions

1. Start by making the Asian Peach Glaze. In a saucepan over medium heat, combine the peach preserves, sweet chili sauce, sriracha sauce, and lime juice and mix well.

2. Turn to medium-low heat, cover with a lid, and cook for 30 minutes. Stir often.

3. Turn the heat off, add cilantro, and set aside until ready to use.

4. Set up the grill (or smoker) for indirect heat at 225°F. Use hickory, pecan, or any fruitwood for smoking.

5. Apply the Main Street Rib Rub evenly over the spareribs and place them on the grill.

6. Smoke for 3 hours.

7. Wrap the spareribs with heavy-duty aluminum foil and put them back on the smoker.

8. Cook for 2 hours in the wrapped foil.

9. Remove the ribs from the foil and place back on the smoker.

10. Cook for 1 hour. In the final 10 minutes of cooking, brush the glaze on the ribs.

11. Remove the ribs from the smoker and allow rest for 10 minutes or until cool enough to handle.

12. Cut the ribs into individual bones, drizzle the glaze over the ribs, and serve.

SPICY DRY RUBBED RIBS

Serves: 4
Total time: 6½ hours

Ingredients
1 rack whole spareribs, untrimmed

Spicy Rib Rub
2 tbsp. paprika

1 tsp. cayenne pepper

1 tsp. chipotle pepper

1 tsp. ancho pepper

1 tsp. crushed red pepper flakes

1 tsp. seasoned salt

½ tbsp. garlic powder

½ tbsp. onion powder

½ tbsp. ground cumin

½ tsp. dry mustard

1 tsp. parsley

½ tsp. coriander

Instructions
1. Combine all Spicy Rib Rub ingredients in a bowl and set aside until ready to use.

2. Set up the grill (or smoker) for indirect heat at 225°F. Use hickory, pecan, or any fruitwood for smoking.

3. Apply the Spicy Rib Rub evenly over the ribs and place them on the grill. Smoke for 3 hours.

4. Wrap the ribs tightly with heavy-duty aluminum foil.

5. Cook for 2½ hours.

6. Unwrap the ribs and place them directly on the cooker. Cook for another hour.

7. Remove the ribs from the smoker and place them on a platter to rest for 10 minutes.

8. Slice and serve immediately. Dust the ribs with a little more heat.

SWEETBURST SEASONED PORK RIBS

Serves: 2
Total time: 6 hours

Ingredients
1 rack pork spareribs, St. Louis style

SweetBurst Rub
3 tbsp. turbinado sugar

2 tbsp. white sugar

2 tbsp. paprika

1 tbsp. seasoned salt

1 tsp. onion powder

1 tsp. garlic powder

1 tsp. black pepper

1 tsp. dried parsley

Instructions
1. Combine all SweetBurst Rub ingredients in a bowl and mix well. Store in an airtight container or a storage bag until ready to use.

2. Set up the grill (or smoker) for indirect heat at 225°F. Use hickory, pecan, or any fruitwood for smoking.

3. Apply the SweetBurst Rub evenly over spareribs and place it on the grill. Smoke for 3 hours.

4. Wrap the rack of ribs in heavy-duty aluminum foil. Cook for 2 hours.

5. Unwrap the ribs and place the rack back on the cooker for 1 hour.

6. Remove the ribs from the cooker and rest for 10 minutes or until it is cool enough to handle.

7. Slice the rack into individual bones and serve immediately.

CHAPTER 2

BABY BACK RIB RECIPES

ADOBO PORK RIBS

Serves: 2
Total time: 2½ hours

Ingredients

1 rack of baby back ribs
½ cup soy sauce
12 cloves of garlic, crushed
10 bay leaves
2 tbsp. whole black peppercorns
1 cup water
Oil, for frying
½ cup white vinegar
Fresh cracked pepper, to taste

Instructions

1. Cut the ribs into individual bones.

2. Combine half the amount of soy sauce, garlic, bay leaves, and peppercorns in a large storage bag.

3. Place all the rib bones in the storage bag and marinate for at least 24 hours and up to 5 days.

4. Set up the cooker for high heat grilling at 500°F.

5. Grill all sides of the ribs and place them in a foil pan.

6. Combine the other half of the soy sauce, garlic, bay leaves, and peppercorns with the ribs, add the water, and lightly stir.

7. Cook using indirect heat at 300°F for 2 hours.

8. In a fryer, deep fry the ribs for 5 minutes at 375°F.

9. Add vinegar to the juices in the foil pan and stir.

10. Coat the individual ribs in the foil pan sauce, add pepper to taste, and serve immediately.

BACON AND JALAPEÑO-CRUSTED RIBS WITH SRIRACHA CHEESE SAUCE

Serves: 2
Total time: 4 hours

Ingredients

2-lb. rack baby back ribs
2 tbsp. Main Street Rib Rub (page 192)

Sriracha Cheese Sauce

1 tbsp. canola oil
1 tbsp. all-purpose flour
1 cup milk
½ cup cheddar cheese, finely shredded
¼ cup sriracha sauce

Other Ingredients

1 lb. bacon, cooked and chopped
2 whole jalapeños, diced
2 tbsp. brown sugar

Instructions

1. Set up grill for indirect heat at 225°F. Use any fruitwood, hickory, or pecan for smoke in this recipe.

2. Apply Main Street Rib Rub evenly over the ribs.

3. Smoke ribs for 2 hours.

4. While ribs are smoking, make the Sriracha Cheese Sauce. In a saucepan, heat up the oil over medium heat and then add the flour. Combine well.

5. Add milk slowly and stir until smooth. When the mixture starts to boil, turn the heat down to low and slowly stir in all the cheese.

6. Pour in the sririacha sauce and mix well.

7. Stir until all the cheese is melted; the sauce will thicken as it cools. (You can refrigerate the leftover sauce for up to 4 days.)

8. After ribs have smoked for 2 hours, wrap ribs tightly in heavy-duty aluminum foil and cook for 1½ hours.

9. Unwrap the ribs and discard foil. Mix the bacon crumbles with diced jalapeños and brown sugar and sprinkle on top of the ribs. Cook for 30 minutes.

10. Top the ribs with the rest of the sauce.

11. Slice and serve.

BACON-CRUSTED MAPLE DIJON RIBS

Serves: 2
Total time: 4 hours

Ingredients

2-lb. rack baby back ribs

2 tbsp. Main Street Rib Rub (page 192)

½ cup maple syrup

1 tbsp. whole-grain Dijon mustard

1 lb. bacon, cooked and chopped

Instructions

1. Set up grill for indirect heat at 225°F. Use any hickory, pecan, or fruitwood, for smoke in this recipe.

2. Apply Main Street Rib Rub evenly over the ribs.

3. Smoke ribs for 2 hours.

4. In a bowl, combine the maple syrup and Dijon mustard together and mix well. Set the sauce aside at room temperature.

5. Wrap ribs tightly in heavy-duty aluminum foil and cook for 1½ hours.

6. Unwrap the ribs, discard foil, and apply ½ of the maple Dijon sauce over the ribs. Smash the bacon crumbles on top of the ribs and cook for 30 minutes.

7. Top the ribs with the rest of the sauce.

8. Slice and serve.

BACON-CRUSTED, PUMPKIN-GLAZED BABY BACK RIBS

Serves: 2
Total time: 4 hours

Ingredients

2-lb. rack baby back ribs
1 lb. bacon, cooked and chopped
2 tbsp. Main Street Rib Rub (page 192)

Pumpkin Glaze

½ cup brown sugar
1 tsp. pumpkin spice
1 stick unsalted butter
½ cup ketchup
2 tbsp. white vinegar
½ tsp. onion powder
½ tsp. garlic powder
½ tsp. mustard powder

Instructions

1. Set up grill for indirect heat at 225°F. Use any hickory, pecan, or fruitwood, for smoke in this recipe.

2. Apply Main Street Rib Rub evenly over the ribs.

3. Smoke ribs for 2 hours.

4. Combine the pumpkin glaze ingredients in a saucepan on medium low heat. Simmer for 30 minutes and stir often. Turn off and allow to sit at room temperature until ready to use.

5. Wrap ribs tightly in heavy-duty aluminum foil and cook for 1½ hours.

6. Unwrap the ribs, discard foil, and apply ½ of the pumpkin glaze over the ribs. Smash the bacon crumbles on top of the ribs and cook for 30 minutes.

7. Top the ribs with the rest of the sauce.

8. Slice and serve.

BACON-WRAPPED BABY BACK RIBS

Serves: 2
Total time: 4½ hours

> Why not? I've seen whole chickens and alligators wrapped in bacon. Just add this to the list of ridiculous reasons why my cardiologist weeps uncontrollably when he sees me.

Ingredients

2-lb. rack baby back ribs
2 tbsp. Main Street Rib Rub (page 192)
1 lb. bacon, sliced
½ cup Hwy K Rib Sauce (page 193)

Instructions

1. Set up grill for indirect heat at 225°F. Use any hickory, pecan, or fruitwood for smoke in this recipe.

2. Apply Main Street Rib Rub evenly over the ribs.

3. Smoke ribs for 2 hours.

4. Make a bacon weave by laying strips in a gridlike pattern, weaving over and under each other, like a basket.

5. After the first 2 hours of smoking, place the rack meat side down on top of the bacon weave. Wrap the edges of the bacon weave over the bone side of the ribs. Place the ribs, meat side up, back on the smoker. Cook for 2 hours.

6. Ribs are done when the bacon looks crispy and cooked through.

7. Cover the ribs with Hwy K Rib Sauce and cook for another 30 minutes.

8. Slice and serve.

Tip

Using thin bacon strips will help ensure that the bacon cooks all the way through. Thick-cut slices tend to be rubbery and require more time in the cooker, potentially making you overcook the ribs.

BLOWTORCH RIBS

The GrillinFools are a few crazy guys, led by Scott Thomas, who showed me the ropes on turning bad barbecue into great entertainment for my barbecue blog. He's cooked way more legendary recipes than bad ones. These baby back ribs are his version from pitmaster great Skip Steele at Bogart's Smokehouse in St. Louis. Check out www.grillinfools.com.

Serves: 6
Total time: 2½ hours

Ingredients
2-lb. rack baby back ribs

Brine
1 quart apple juice
¼ cup salt
2 tbsp. minced garlic
1 tsp. fresh cracked black pepper

Rub
2 tbsp. garlic powder
2 tbsp. turbinado sugar
2 tbsp. pumpkin pie spice
1 tbsp. sweet paprika

Glaze
2 tbsp. apple jelly
2 tbsp. apricot preserves
2 tbsp. hot pepper jelly
2 tsp. Worcestershire sauce

Instructions
1. Combine the Brine ingredients in a storage bag and slosh around until the salt is dissolved.

2. Remove the membrane off the back of the ribs.

3. Place the ribs in the bag with the brine and refrigerate overnight.

4. Combine the Rub ingredients in a bowl. Give the bone side of the ribs a dusting to a coating (your preference). Flip the ribs and repeat on the meat side.

5. Prepare the grill for 2-zone grilling (or indirect grilling) with coals and smoke wood—use chunks of pecan wood on one side and nothing on the other. Target temperature of the inside of the grill is 275–300°F.

6. Place the ribs on the side of the grill with no heat and close the lid.

7. When the meat pulls back from the bone about a half inch (about 2 hours at this temperature), remove from grill and make the Glaze.

8. Combine the Glaze ingredients in a bowl and put in the microwave for about 90 seconds to liquify the gelatin. Mix well.

9. Flip the slabs over to the bone side and slather with the Glaze.

10. Blast the glaze with a couple minutes of the blowtorch (making sure the flame is blue and not orange) by constantly rocking the flame slowly back and forth across the glaze (optional).

11. Flip over to the meat side and smear with the glaze.

12. Blast with the torch on the meat side.

13. Once a sugary crust is achieved on all the slabs, remove from the heat. Allow to rest for five minutes before slicing and serving.

CAJUN BABY BACK RIBS

Serves: 2
Total time: 4 hours

Ingredients
1 rack of baby back ribs

Waterboy Rib Rub
1 tsp. red pepper flakes
1 tsp. dried thyme leaves
1 tsp. dried oregano leaves
½ tsp. dried rosemary
2 tbsp. paprika
1 tsp. garlic salt
1 tsp. Lawry's seasoned salt
½ tbsp. ground cumin
1 tsp. cayenne pepper
½ tsp. ground black pepper

Instructions
1. Set up the grill (or smoker) for indirect heat at 225°F. Use hickory, pecan, or any fruitwood for smoking.

2. To make the Waterboy Rib Rub, use a coffee grinder to coarsely grind red pepper flakes, thyme, oregano, and rosemary. Do not grind too finely.

3. In a bowl, combine all the Waterboy Rib Rub ingredients and mix well. Store in an airtight container or a storage bag until ready to use.

4. Apply the Waterboy Rib Rub evenly over the baby back ribs and place them on the grill.

5. Smoke for 2 hours.

6. Wrap the ribs tightly in heavy-duty aluminum foil and place back on the cooker.

7. Cook for 1½ hours.

8. Unwrap the ribs and cook for 30 minutes.

9. Rest the rack of ribs until they are cool enough to handle, about 10 minutes.

10. Slice the ribs into individual bones and serve immediately. Apply extra Waterboy Rib Rub while serving.

CHAR SIU PORK RIBS

Serves: 2
Total time: 3 hours

Ingredients

1 rack baby back ribs

Marinade

1 cup soy sauce

¼ cup honey whiskey

¼ cup hoisin sauce

2 tbsp. ginger ale

½ cup dark brown sugar

¼ cup red wine vinegar

2 tsp. red food coloring

4 toasted star anise pods

Instructions

1. Combine all Marinade ingredients in a large storage bag. Reserve 1 cup of marinade.

2. Slice the ribs into single bones.

3. Marinate the single ribs portions at least overnight and up to 48 hours.

4. Set up cooker for indirect heat at 300°F.

5. Place ribs on the grill and cook for 2 hours.

6. Place ribs in a foil pan and cover with aluminum foil. Cook for 1 hour.

7. Remove ribs from pan and cook on the grill for 30 minutes. Baste the ribs with reserve marinade.

8. Ribs are ready when meat easily separates from the bone. Serve immediately.

GINGER-GLAZED BABY BACK RIBS

Serves: 2
Total time: 4 hours

Ingredients

1 rack baby back ribs
¼ cup pineapple juice
Sesame seeds, toasted

Five-Spice Rub

2 tsp. Chinese five-spice seasoning
2 tbsp. paprika
2 tsp. sugar
2 tsp. crushed red pepper flakes
1 tsp. garlic powder
1 tsp. onion powder
1 tsp. kosher salt

Ginger Glaze

½ cup Bragg Liquid Aminos (or soy sauce)
½ cup honey
¼ cup peeled and grated gingerroot
2 tbsp. brown sugar
1 tbsp. white vinegar
4 garlic cloves
¼ cup water

Instructions

1. Set up grill for indirect heat at 225°F. Use hickory, pecan, or any fruitwood for smoke.

2. Mix all the Five-Spice Rub ingredients together in a bowl and apply the rub evenly over the ribs. Let the ribs sit for 10 minutes to absorb the spices.

3. Place the ribs in the smoker and cook for 2 hours.

4. Remove the ribs from the smoker and make a foil wrap. Place the ribs meat side up in the foil wrap and pour the pineapple juice over the ribs. Wrap the foil tightly and place the ribs back on the smoker (meat side up).

5. Cook for 1½ hours.

6. In a saucepan over medium-low heat, add all the Ginger Glaze ingredients. Cook for 1 hour, checking and stirring occasionally. Add more water if necessary. Keep at room temperature when it's done.

7. Once ribs have smoked for 1½ hours, remove from smoker.

8. Set up grill for direct heat at 600°F.

9. Grill the ribs over high heat, basting with the glaze. The ribs are ready after 5–10 minutes or when the ribs are perfectly caramelized.

10. Slice the ribs into individual bones and garnish with sesame seeds.

11. Serve immediately.

HIGH HEAT BABY BACK RIBS

Serves: 2
Total time: 2½ hours

Ingredients

1 rack baby back ribs, whole
¼ cup Main Street Rib Rub (page 192)

Foil Wrap

3 tbsp. pineapple juice
3 tbsp. unsalted butter
¼ cup soy sauce
1 tbsp. brown sugar
½ tbsp. cayenne pepper

Instructions

1. Set up the grill (or smoker) for indirect heat at 350°F. Use hickory and/or peach wood.

2. Apply the Main Street Rib Rub evenly over the baby back ribs and place them on the grill.

3. Smoke for 1 hour.

4. Wrap the Foil Wrap ingredients and ribs tightly with heavy-duty aluminum foil. Place the ribs back on the smoker.

5. Cook for 1 hour.

6. Remove from the cooker, unwrap from aluminum foil (reserving liquid), and cook for another 30 minutes. Brush with the liquids from the wrap the last 10 minutes of cooking.

7. Remove the ribs from the smoker and rest on a platter for 5 minutes. Brush more Foil Wrap liquids over the ribs and slice the ribs into individual bones.

8. Serve immediately.

PB&J BABY BACK RIBS

Serves: 4
Total time: 5 hours

Ingredients
1 rack baby back ribs

Peanut Spice Rub
⅓ cup roasted peanuts

3 tbsp. turbinado sugar

2 tsp. chipotle powder

1 tbsp. chili powder

1 tsp. dried basil

1 tsp. ground cumin

2 tsp. black pepper

1 tbsp. kosher salt

Foil Wrap
⅓ cup grape jelly

2 tbsp. ketchup

2 tbsp. soy sauce

2 sprigs of thyme, fresh

Instructions
1. Set up the grill (or smoker) for indirect heat at 225°F. Use hickory, pecan, or any fruitwood for smoking.

2. Make the Peanut Spice Rub. Use a coffee grinder to pulverize the peanuts into tiny pieces, but not into a powder.

3. In a bowl, combine all Peanut Spice Rub ingredients and mix well. If not using immediately, store in an airtight container or a storage bag.

4. Apply the Peanut Spice Rub evenly over baby back ribs and place ribs on the grill.

5. Smoke for 2 hours.

6. Mix the Foil Wrap ingredients together in a bowl. Use a sheet of heavy-duty foil and place the Foil Wrap glaze in the center of the foil. Place the meat side of the ribs on top of the Foil Wrap ingredients. Wrap the rack of ribs tightly in the heavy-duty aluminum foil.

7. Cook for 1½ hours.

8. Unwrap the ribs and place the rack back on the cooker for 30 minutes. Reserve the glaze from the Foil Wrap.

9. Remove the ribs from the cooker and rest for 10 minutes or until cool enough to handle.

10. Slice the rack into individual bones, drizzle jelly glaze over the ribs, and serve immediately.

PINEAPPLE CHIPOTLE GLAZED BBR

Serves: 2
Total time: 5 hours

Ingredients
1 rack baby back ribs
2 tbsp. Main Street Rib Rub (page 192)

Pineapple Chipotle Glaze
¼ cup pineapple jelly
½ cup chopped fresh pineapple
2 chipotle peppers in adobo sauce, chopped
¼ cup ketchup
2 tbsp. soy sauce
2 tbsp. apple cider vinegar
½ tsp. liquid smoke

Instructions
1. Set up the grill (or smoker) for indirect heat at 225°F. Use hickory, pecan, or any fruitwood for smoking.

2. Apply the Main Street Rib Rub evenly over baby back ribs and place ribs on the grill.

3. Smoke for 2 hours.

4. In the meantime, make the Pineapple Chipotle Glaze. In a saucepan, combine all glaze ingredients and cook on medium low heat for 30 minutes.

5. Use an immersion blender or food processor to blend the sauce until smooth. Cook for 10 minutes. Set aside until ready to use.

6. Wrap the rack of ribs with a sheet of heavy-duty aluminum foil. Cook for 1½ hours.

7. Unwrap the ribs and place the rack back on the cooker for 30 minutes. Baste the ribs with the glaze every 10 minutes.

8. Remove the ribs from the cooker and rest for 10 minutes or until it is cool enough to handle.

9. Slice the rack into individual bones, drizzle glaze over the ribs, and serve immediately.

RIB COCKTAIL

Serves: 2
Total time: 5 hours

> I was inspired by watching a TV show that was all about state fair food. What a great way to share ribs among friends and family. How would you like to be served one of these by the poolside? Dreams do come true!

Ingredients

1 rack baby back ribs
1 cup coleslaw (page 197)
2 tbsp. Main Street Rib Rub (page 192)
Hwy K Rib Sauce, to taste (page 193)

Instructions

1. Set up the grill (or smoker) for indirect heat at 225°F. Use hickory, pecan, or any fruitwood for smoking.

2. Apply the Main Street Rib Rub evenly over the ribs and place them on the grill.

3. Smoke for 2 hours.

4. Wrap the ribs tightly with heavy-duty aluminum foil and put back on the smoker.

5. Cook for 2 hours.

6. Unwrap the ribs and put them back on the smoker.

7. Cook for 30 minutes.

8. Remove the ribs from the smoker and rest for 5 minutes or until cool enough to handle.

9. Use either a margarita glass or martini glass and stick 4 rib bones pointing upward in it. Put a scoop of coleslaw in the center of the glass. Top the cocktail with rib rub and rib sauce. Garnish is optional.

10. Serve immediately.

SOUTHWEST BBR

Serves: 4
Total time: 5 hours

Ingredients

1 rack baby back ribs

Southwest Rib Rub

3 tbsp. chili powder

1 tbsp. ground cumin

1 tbsp. paprika

2 tsp. black pepper

1 tsp. ground coriander

1 tsp. ground cayenne pepper

1 tbsp. crushed red pepper

2 tsp. oregano

1 tsp. garlic salt

1 tsp. onion powder

Instructions

1. Combine all Southwest Rib Rub ingredients in a bowl and mix well. Store in an airtight container or a storage bag until ready to use.

2. Set up the grill (or smoker) for indirect heat at 225°F. Use hickory, pecan, or any fruitwood for smoking.

3. Apply the Southwest Rib Rub evenly over baby back ribs and place on the grill.

4. Smoke for 2 hours.

5. Wrap the rack of ribs in heavy-duty aluminum foil.

6. Cook for 1½ hours.

7. Unwrap the ribs and place the rack back on the cooker for 30 minutes.

8. Remove the ribs from the cooker and rest for 10 minutes or until cool enough to handle.

9. Slice the rack into individual bones and serve immediately.

SPICY APRICOT GLAZED PORK RIBS

Serves: 4
Total time: 5 hours

Ingredients
1 rack baby back ribs
2 tbsp. Main Street Rib Rub (page 192)

Spicy Apricot Glaze
¾ cup apricot preserves
¼ cup adobo sauce (from chipotles in a can)
½ tsp. garlic powder
½ tsp. mustard powder
½ tsp. cumin
2 tbsp. white vinegar

Instructions
1. Set up the grill (or smoker) for indirect heat at 225°F. Use hickory, pecan, or any fruitwood for smoking.

2. Apply the Main Street Rib Rub evenly over the baby back ribs and place them on the grill.

3. Smoke for 2 hours.

4. In the meantime, make the Spicy Apricot Glaze. In a saucepan over medium heat, combine all ingredients in the pan and mix well.

5. Turn the heat down to medium low, cover with a lid, and simmer for 30 minutes. Stir often.

6. Turn off the heat and set aside until ready to use.

7. Wrap the ribs with heavy-duty aluminum foil and put the rack back on the smoker.

8. Cook for 2 hours in the foil.

9. Unwrap the ribs from the foil and cook on the smoker for 30 minutes. Baste with the glaze the last 10 minutes of cook time.

10. Remove the BBR from the smoker and rest for 5 minutes.

11. Slice the ribs into individual bones and serve. Drizzle the glaze over the ribs.

SWEET AND SPICY MEXICAN RIBS

Serves: 4
Total time: 5 hours

Ingredients
1 rack baby back ribs
2 tbsp. All Purpose Meat Rub (page 192)

Sweet and Spicy Sauce
6 whole ancho chiles, dried
4 whole pasilla chiles, dried
3 cups water
2 tbsp. Mexican oregano
1 tbsp. cumin
2 tbsp. white vinegar
4 cloves garlic, roasted
1 tbsp. kosher salt
2 tbsp. canola oil
2 medium piloncillo cones (or 2 cups brown sugar)

Instructions
1. Set up the grill (or smoker) for indirect heat at 225°F. Use hickory, pecan, or any fruitwood for smoking.

2. Apply the All Purpose Meat Rub evenly over the baby back ribs and place them on the grill.

3. Smoke for 2 hours.

4. In the meantime, make the Sweet and Spicy Sauce. Lightly roast the dried chiles by grilling them over direct high heat for a few seconds on each side. Avoid burning them as that will leave a bitter taste.

5. Soak the chiles in hot water until soft. Reserve the chile-flavored water for upcoming steps.

6. Remove the seeds from the chiles and put the skin in a food processor.

7. Add 1 cup of water to the food processor. Also add oregano, cumin, vinegar, garlic, and salt. Blend until smooth.

8. Use a fine mesh strainer to remove the large food particles.

9. Add canola oil to a saucepan over medium heat and wait for the oil to shimmer. Pour the strained sauce into the saucepan to cook out the bitterness. Cook about 5 minutes.

10. Add the piloncillo cones, turn down to medium-low heat, cover with a lid, and simmer the sauce for 1 hour. Add chile water, if necessary, to thin out the sauce.

11. Once the cones are dissolved, remove from the heat and set aside until ready to use.

12. Once the ribs have smoked for 2 hours, remove from grill or smoker, wrap tightly with heavy-duty aluminum foil, and place them back on the cooker.

13. Cook for 2 hours.

14. Remove the ribs from the foil and place them back on the cooker.

15. Cook unwrapped for 30 minutes.

16. Remove the ribs from the smoker and let rest for 5 minutes.

17. Cut the ribs into individual bones and drizzle them with the Sweet and Spicy Sauce. Serve immediately.

CHAPTER 3

BEEF SHORT RIB (BONE-IN) RECIPES

7 PEPPER BEEF RIBS

Serves: 3–4
Total time: 5½ hours

Ingredients
1 rack beef short ribs
Cooking spray

7 Pepper Rub
1 tsp. each of whole black, red, green, and white
  peppercorns
1 tsp. dried and chopped red bell pepper
1 tsp. red pepper flakes
1 tsp. ground ancho chile
1 tbsp. garlic salt
1 tsp. seasoned salt
1 tbsp. onion powder

Instructions
1. Set up the grill (or smoker) for indirect heat at 225°F. Use hickory, pecan, or any fruitwood for smoking.

2. Make the 7 Pepper Rub. In a coffee grinder, put in all the peppercorns, bell peppers, and red pepper flakes. Grind until you get a coarse texture.

3. Mix all the ingredients together in a bowl.

4. Apply the 7 Pepper Rub evenly over the short ribs and place them on the grill.

5. Smoke for 2½ hours.

6. Wrap the short ribs tightly with heavy-duty aluminum foil. Place back on the grill and cook for 2 hours.

7. Unwrap the ribs and cook for another 1 hour on the grill.

8. Slice and serve short ribs immediately.

BARBACOA

Serves: 4
Total time: 5 hours

> Here's my take on a simple and rustic approach for cooking massive whole beef short ribs. Every Mexican grocery store should carry fresh banana leaves, sometimes in the freezer section. If not, aluminum foil works just as well, but I love the banana leaves more for presentation . . . they just look cool!

Ingredients

1 rack beef short ribs
Fresh banana leaves

Barbacoa Beef Rub

2 tbsp. ground chile de arbol
1 tsp. garlic salt
1 tsp. onion powder
1 pk. Goya Sazón

Instructions

1. Set up the grill (or smoker) for indirect heat at 225°F. Use hickory, pecan, or any fruitwood for smoking.

2. Combine all Barbacoa Beef Rub ingredients in a bowl and mix well. Set aside until ready to use.

3. Apply the Barbacoa Beef Rub evenly over the short ribs and place them on the grill.

4. Smoke for 1 hour.

5. Wrap short ribs in banana leaves, then place it in a foil pan and cover with a sheet of foil.

6. Braise for 3 hours, until tender.

7. Unwrap the beef short ribs and cook for 1 hour.

8. Slice into single servings and serve short ribs immediately.

BARBECUED BEEF RIBS

Serves: 6
Total time: 3½ hours

Ingredients
2 racks beef back ribs
2 tbsp. oil

Beef Rub
2 tsp. kosher salt
2 tsp. black pepper
1 tsp. garlic powder
1 tsp. Mexican chili powder
1 tsp. dried oregano

Beef Mop
¼ cup beef stock
2 tbsp. cider vinegar
2 tbsp. beer
2 tbsp. ketchup
2 tbsp. oil
½ tbsp. Worcestershire sauce
½ tbsp. hot sauce
½ tbsp. Beef Rub

One of my favorite BBQ blogs and recipe sites was founded by Chris Grove, who created this recipe. He's a fellow Big Green Egg grill user, so he's no bad egg (you see what I did there?). Great beefy flavor profile in this recipe. Check out www.nibblemethis.com.

Instructions

1. Set up cooker for indirect heat at 300°F. Use oak wood for smoke flavor.

2. Mix the Beef Rub ingredients together.

3. Whisk Beef Mop ingredients together.

4. Apply oil and season the ribs on both sides with the Beef Rub.

5. Cook the ribs over indirect heat for 1 hour on each side. Mop or baste the ribs with the Beef Mop every 30 minutes.

6. Place each rib bone side up on a double sheet of foil with 2 tbsp. of Beef Mop. Seal tightly and put back on the grill until tender, about 45–60 minutes.

7. Carefully remove from foil and place back on the grill until the color darkens, about 30 minutes.

BEEF RIBS WITH CHIMICHURRI SAUCE

Serves: 2
Total time: 4 hours

Ingredients
2 lbs. beef short ribs, English cut

Beef Rub
¼ tsp. ground fennel

¼ tsp. ground celery salt

¼ tsp. ground chile de arbol

1 tbsp. garlic salt

1 tbsp. pepper

½ tbsp. onion powder

½ tbsp. white sugar

1 tsp. Hungarian paprika

1 tsp. Accent

Chimichurri Sauce
4 cloves garlic

2 tbsp. chopped yellow onions

1 cup fresh flat-leaf parsley

1 cup fresh cilantro

¼ cup fresh oregano leaves

½ cup olive oil

2 tbsp. red wine vinegar

1 tbsp. freshly squeezed lime juice

2 tbsp. kosher salt

2 tbsp. crushed red pepper flakes

Instructions
1. Set up the smoker or grill for indirect cooking at 250°F

2. Mix Beef Rub ingredients together in a bowl.

3. Apply the Beef Rub on the short ribs.

4. Use hickory wood for smoke and place the short ribs on the smoker.

5. Cook for 2 hours at 250 degrees°F

6. In the meantime, make the Chimichurri Sauce. In a food processor (or blender), pulse the garlic and onion until finely chopped.

7. Add the parsley, cilantro, and oregano and pulse briefly, until finely chopped (not pureed).

8. Place the mixture in a bowl. Add the olive oil, red wine vinegar, and lime juice and mix well by hand.

9. Season with salt and red pepper flakes. Store in the refrigerator until ready to serve.

10. Place all the short ribs in a small foil pan and cover with a sheet of aluminum foil.

11. Cook for another 1½ hours in the foil pan, until tender.

12. Remove the short ribs from the foil pan and place back on the cooker, discarding the foil pan and its contents.

13. Cook the short ribs for another 30 minutes, meat side up.

14. Remove the short ribs from the cooker and serve with Chimichurri Sauce.

BEEF SHORT RIBS WITH GARLICPEÑO RUB

Serves: 4
Total time: 5 hours

Ingredients

2 lbs. beef short ribs, whole
Garlicpeño Rub
3 sprigs thyme, fresh
3 sprigs oregano, fresh
3 tbsp. olive oil

Garlicpeño Rub

3 tbsp. garlic salt
1 tsp. dried ground jalapeño
1 tbsp. onion powder
1 tbsp. dried ground roasted garlic
½ tbsp. ground green peppercorns

Instructions

1. Set up the grill (or smoker) for indirect heat at 225°F. Use hickory, pecan, or any fruitwood for smoking.

2. Combine all Garlicpeño Rub ingredients in a bowl and mix well.

3. Apply the seasoning rub evenly over the short ribs and place them on the grill.

4. Smoke for 1½ hours.

5. Tear off a sheet of heavy-duty aluminum foil long enough to cover the short ribs. Wrap the beef short ribs with the fresh thyme and oregano in the foil.

6. Braise for 3 hours until tender.

7. Remove the beef short ribs from the smoker and rest until cool enough to handle.

8. On a cutting board, chop up the herbs taken from the foiled short ribs. Pour the olive oil on the board and combine the herbs and oil.

9. Place the beef short ribs meat side down on the cutting board. Make sure the meat comes in contact with as much olive oil mixture as possible. Cut the ribs into individual bones.

10. Serve short ribs immediately.

CHERRY BALSAMIC BEEF SHORT RIBS

Serves: 3
Total time: 4 hours

Ingredients

2 lbs. beef short ribs, 2-inch English cut

2 tbsp. Beef Rub (page 192)

1 cup cherry preserves

½ cup balsamic vinegar

2 sprigs fresh thyme

Instructions

1. Set up the grill (or smoker) for indirect heat at 225°F. Use hickory, pecan, or any fruitwood for smoking.

2. Apply the Beef Rub evenly over the short ribs and place them on the grill.

3. Smoke for 1½ hours.

4. In a foil pan, combine the remaining ingredients and place the short ribs in the pan. Cover the foil pan with heavy-duty aluminum foil and put it on the smoker.

5. Braise for 2 hours or until tender.

6. Remove the short ribs from the foil pan and cook on the smoker for 30 minutes.

7. Remove the beef short ribs from the smoker and dip them in the foil pan sauce.

8. Serve immediately.

COFFEE-CRUSTED BEEF SHORT RIBS

Serves: 2
Total time: 4 hours

Ingredients

1 lb. English 2-inch cut beef short ribs

Coffee Beef Rub

2 tbsp. Instant coffee

1 tbsp. ground ancho chile

1 tbsp. ground chile de arbol

½ tsp. cumin

1 tsp. black pepper

1 tsp. kosher salt

Wrapping Glaze

2 tbsp. olive oil

6 cloves garlic, crushed

¼ cup honey

Instructions

1. Set up grill (or smoker) for indirect heat at 300°F. Use hickory, pecan, or any fruitwood.

2. Apply the Coffee Beef Rub all over the ribs. Smoke the beef short ribs for 1 hour.

3. Place the ribs in a foil pan and pour in the Wrapping Glaze ingredients. Cover with heavy-duty aluminum foil and cook for 2 hours or until tender.

4. Brush the glaze on all the ribs and serve immediately.

HIGH HEAT BEEF SHORT RIBS WITH BLEU CHEESE COMPOUND

Serves: 3
Total time: 4 hours

Ingredients

1 rack beef short ribs, whole
2 tbsp. Beef Rub (page 192)

Bleu Cheese Compound

1 stick unsalted butter, softened
3 tbsp. bleu cheese crumbles
2 cloves roasted garlic
1 tbsp. minced red onion
½ tsp. Worcestershire sauce

Instructions

1. In a bowl, combine all the Bleu Cheese Compound ingredients and mix well.

2. Pour the butter compound into the center of a sheet of plastic wrap.

3. Shape the compound into a 1-inch diameter log. Wrap tightly and place it in the freezer for 30 minutes.

4. Move the butter log to the fridge until ready to use.

5. Set up the grill (or smoker) for indirect heat at 300°F. Use hickory, pecan, or any fruitwood for smoking.

6. Apply the Beef Rub evenly over the short ribs and place them on the grill.

7. Smoke for 1½ hours.

8. Wrap beef short ribs with a sheet of heavy-duty aluminum foil.

9. Cook for 2 more hours.

10. Unwrap the beef short ribs and cook on the smoker for 30 minutes.

11. Slice the butter compound into ½-inch discs.

12. Remove the beef ribs from the grill and rest on a serving plate. Put 2 discs of butter compound on the hot beef ribs. Rest for 10 minutes and let the compound melt.

13. Slice and serve short ribs.

PORTER BRAISED SHORT RIBS

Serves: 4
Total time: 5 hours

Ingredients

3 lbs. beef short ribs, English cut
2 bottles (12 fl. oz. each) of porter craft beer
   (Smoked or Whiskey Vanilla are excellent too)
½ cup soy sauce
2 tbsp. Asian chili garlic sauce
1 tbsp. Worcestershire sauce
2 sprigs fresh rosemary
6 cloves garlic, crushed
1 large onion, rough chop
3 whole carrots, rough chop
4 stalks celery, rough chop
All Purpose Meat Rub (page 192)
Kosher salt and pepper, to taste

Instructions

1. In a bowl, combine all All Purpose Meat Rub ingredients and mix well. Set aside until ready to use.

2. Set up the grill (or smoker) for indirect heat at 225°F. Use hickory, pecan, or any fruitwood for smoking.

3. Apply the meat rub evenly over the short ribs and place them on the grill.

4. Smoke for 1½ hours.

5. In a foil pan, combine the remaining ingredients and place the short ribs on top. Cover the foil pan with heavy-duty aluminum foil.

6. Braise for 3 hours until tender.

7. Set up the grill for direct heat at 600°F.

8. Sear the short ribs over high heat until a flavor crust develops.

9. Use a stick blender or food processor to blend the braising liquid until smooth. Strain liquid with a fine mesh strainer.

10. Serve short ribs immediately with a side of the braising juice.

CHAPTER 4

OFF THE BONE RIB RECIPES

50/50 FRANKENBURGER

Serves: 4
Total time: 45 minutes

Ingredients

2 lbs. ground chuck

2 lbs. ground pork

2 lbs. smoked pork rib meat, shredded

½ cup Hwy K Rib Sauce (page 193)

4 brioche buns, buttered

8 strips of bacon, cooked

4 eggs, fried

Honey Mustard Mayo Sauce

½ cup mayonnaise

¼ cup Dijon mustard

3 tbsp. honey

1 tsp. lemon juice

Kosher salt and pepper, to taste

Instructions

1. Combine all Honey Mustard Mayo Sauce ingredients in a bowl and mix well.

2. Refrigerate until ready to use. Store in the fridge for up to 4 days.

3. Fire up the grill for a 2-zone set up.

4. Combine the ground chuck and ground pork. Evenly divide the ground meat mixture into 4 balls and form them into patties.

5. Place the patties on the hot side of the grill and cook until the patties are seared and develop a flavor crust. Flip the patties to the cool side of the grill, close the lid, and cook for 12 minutes or until the internal temperature reaches 165°F. Let patties rest for 2 minutes.

6. In a skillet, heat up shredded rib meat with ½ cup of Hwy K Rib Sauce. Cook for 10 minutes or until heated through.

7. Toast the buns and slather the bottom bun with the Honey Mustard Mayo Sauce.

8. Top the bun with a patty, ½ lb. of rib meat, 2 strips of bacon, and 1 fried egg.

9. Put on the top bun and make the other 3 burgers.

10. Serve immediately.

BBQ CHEESESTEAK SANDWICH

Serves: 4
Total time: 25 minutes

Ingredients

1 lb. smoked beef short ribs, cooked and shredded
1 green bell pepper, seeded and sliced
1 cup sliced mushrooms
4 slices provolone cheese
Spicy brown deli mustard
Mayonnaise
Banana peppers
4 white 6-inch sub rolls

Caramelized Onions

1 medium yellow onion, sliced
1 tsp. olive oil
1 tsp. Worcestershire sauce

Instructions

1. Caramelize onion: In a skillet over medium low heat, add oil and onions.

2. Cook for 15 minutes, stirring occasionally.

3. Add Worcestershire sauce and cook for another 15 minutes. Set aside.

4. In a skillet over medium-high heat, cook the pepper, mushrooms, and shredded meat until tender (about 10 minutes). Turn off heat.

5. Squeeze a liberal amount of mustard and mayo on top of the meat mixture. Then spread the onions across the top. Add some banana peppers for a spicy effect.

6. Place cheese on top of the meat mixture and let the residual heat melt the cheese.

7. Open up a sub roll, take a quarter of the meat mixture, and stuff it in a roll

8. Prepare the other 3 sandwiches as such.

9. Serve immediately.

BBQ PORK BURGER

Serves: 2
Total time: 30 minutes

Ingredients

1 lb. leftover pork ribs, cooked and shredded.

1 lb. ground chuck

4 strips of bacon, cooked

½ cup coleslaw (page 197)

½ cup cheddar cheese, shredded

¼ cup Hwy K Rib Sauce (page 193)

2 brioche hamburger buns, lightly toasted

Instructions

1. Set up the grill for indirect heat at 300°F. Use hickory, pecan, or any fruitwood for smoke.

2. Evenly divide the ground chuck into 2 patties. Cook on the hot side for the first 10 minutes with the lid on and vents open.

3. Move the burgers to the cool side of the grill and cook for 6 minutes more, or until the internal temperature reaches 165°F.

4. Scoop half of the coleslaw onto a bottom bun, followed by a burger, 2 strips of bacon, ½ lb. of pulled pork, rib sauce, and ¼ cup of cheese. Cover the burger with the top bun. Optional: hold in place with a skewer down the center of the burger.

5. Make the second burger with the steps above.

6. Serve immediately.

BBQ SPAGHETTI

Serves: 4
Total time: 45 minutes

Ingredients

1 lb. rib meat, cooked
1 lb. spaghetti noodles, cooked
⅓ cup Hwy K Rib Sauce (page 193)
½ cup mozzarella cheese
½ cup cheddar cheese
½ lb. cup ricotta cheese
Fresh parsley, chopped
1 tbsp. Main Street Rib Rub (page 192)

Instructions

1. Preheat the oven at 450°F.

2. In a foil pan, add the meat, noodles, Rib Sauce, and cheeses. Gently toss together.

3. Put the foil pan in the oven for 30 minutes, or until the cheese melts.

4. Remove the foil pan and add more sauce. Sprinkle the parsley and rib rub over the spaghetti and serve immediately.

BBQ SPUD

Serves: 2
Total time: 1 hour

Ingredients

1 lb. rib meat, cooked
2 large Idaho russet potatoes
Cooking spray
2 cups Hwy K Rib Sauce (page 193)
2 tbsp. Main Street Rib Rub (page 192)
½ tsp. garlic salt
½ tsp. seasoned salt
4 bacon strips, cooked
½ cup water
Pickled red onions
Fresh chives, chopped

Coleslaw

2 cups finely shredded cabbage
3 tbsp. mayonnaise
1½ tbsp. apple cider vinegar
2 tbsp. white sugar
Cracked black pepper, to taste

Cheese Sauce

1 tbsp. canola oil
1 tbsp. flour
1 cup milk
½ cup finely shredded cheddar cheese

Instructions

1. Combine all coleslaw ingredients and mix well.

2. Refrigerate for 1 hour. Only use half the coleslaw for this recipe; serve the rest as a side dish.

3. Spray the potatoes with cooking spray and evenly apply 1 tsp. rub, garlic salt, and seasoned salt. Wrap the potatoes in heavy-duty aluminum foil and cook on the grill (or oven) at 350°F for 1 hour.

4. In a saucepan, make the cheese sauce. Heat up the oil on medium heat and then add the flour. Combine well.

5. Add milk slowly and stir until smooth. When the mixture starts to boil, turn the heat down to low and slowly stir in all the cheese.

6. Stir until all the cheese is melted; the sauce will thicken as it cools. Refrigerate the leftovers for up to 4 days.

7. In a skillet over medium heat, add rib meat, 2 tbsp. Rib Rub, ½ cup Rib Sauce, and ½ cup water. Cook until the rib meat starts to shred and the liquids are reduced, about 20–25 minutes.

8. Start building the spud in layers: coleslaw, rib meat, Rib Rub, Rib Sauce, bacon, pickled onions, cheese sauce, and chives.

BEEF SHORT RIB ENCHILADAS

Serves: 4
Total time: 1 hour

Ingredients

1 lb. smoked beef short ribs, shredded

¼ cup diced yellow onions

1 Anaheim chile pepper, roasted and diced

4 corn tortillas

2 cups red enchilada sauce

8 oz. cheddar cheese, shredded

1 oz. green onion, chopped

2 oz. black olives, sliced

Salt and pepper, to taste

Instructions

1. In a saucepan over medium heat, add short ribs, onions, and diced pepper. Season the mixture with salt and pepper. Cook until the onions are soft, then set aside.

2. Warm the tortillas and fill each one with a ¼ lb. of meat, roll into burritos, and place them in a foil pan.

3. Set up the grill for 2-zone indirect cooking at 350°F.

4. Top the tortilla rolls with 1 cup of enchilada sauce, cheese, green onions, and olives. Cover the foil pan with a sheet of aluminum foil. Cook enchiladas on the grill for 30 minutes or until the cheese is melted. Halfway through the cooking process, add the other cup of chile sauce over the enchiladas.

5. Remove the foil pan from the cooker and discard the foil cover. Cool for 5 minutes.

6. Serve immediately.

Note:

Sour cream and guacamole are excellent condiments for enchiladas.

BEER BATTERED RIB BALLS

Servings: 8
Total time: 15 minutes

Ingredients

½ cup smoked rib meat

⅓ cup baked beans

1 tbsp. Main Street Rib Rub (page 192)

⅓ cup shredded cheddar cheese

½ cup flour

½ cup beer

1 tsp. salt

1 tsp. pepper

¼ cup Hwy K Rib Sauce (page 193)

Instructions

1. Heat up oil in a Dutch oven or deep fryer at 375°F.

2. In a large bowl, combine the meat, baked beans, rib rub, and cheese. Mix well.

3. Take a golf ball–size scoop of the meat mixture and roll it into a sphere. Roll the balls around in flour to coat and set aside.

4. Combine the remaining flour, beer, salt, and pepper in a bowl and mix well. The batter should be gravy consistency.

5. Dip the balls in the batter and place them in the deep fryer.

6. Cook for 8–10 minutes until golden brown and delicious.

7. Serve immediately with Rib Sauce on the side.

POCKET PORK SANDWICH

Serves: 4
Total time: 4½ hours

Ingredients

2 lbs. boneless country pork ribs
3 tbsp. McCormick Adobo Seasoning
4 Pillsbury Grands Buttermilk Biscuits, uncooked
Oil for frying

Sofrito

1 medium yellow onion, halved
1 red bell pepper
1 Anaheim pepper
1 head of garlic, roasted
1 bunch of cilantro
1 tbsp. capers
1 tsp. Mexican oregano
⅓ cup olive oil
Kosher salt and pepper, to taste

Instructions

1. To make the Sofrito, set the grill to high heat at 600°F.

2. Roast the onion and peppers. When the peppers are blistered all around, place them in a plastic storage bag and seal. Let the peppers sweat in the bag for 5 minutes, then peel the skin off.

3. Give the roasted onion and peppers a rough chop.

4. Put all Sofrito ingredients (except olive oil) into a food processor and blend until smooth. Add the olive oil at the end through the top while the food processor is on.

5. Use immediately or refrigerate for 3 days.

6. Set up the grill (or smoker) for indirect heat at 225°F. Use hickory, pecan, or any fruitwood for smoking.

7. Apply the Adobo Seasoning evenly over the short ribs and place them on the grill.

8. Smoke for 1 hour.

9. Put the pork in a foil pan and pour the Sofrito over the pork. Cover the foil pan with heavy-duty aluminum foil.

10. Braise for 3 hours, or until tender. Remove from cooker and let rest.

11. Set up the deep fryer at 350°F.

12. Flatten each biscuit dough to about a ¼ inch thickness and fry 1 at a time for 5 minutes or until golden brown and delicious.

13. When the pork is cool enough to touch, pull the meat apart. Allow the pulled meat to absorb the juices in the pan.

14. Make a pocket out of the fried biscuit by slicing through the side and opening it up.

15. Stuff a heaping amount of pork inside the biscuits and serve immediately.

16. Store leftover pork stuffing in a freezer storage bag and freeze up to 1 month or refrigerate for 3 days.

DECONSTRUCTED BEEF RIB TACOS

Serves: 4
Total time: 30 minutes

Ingredients

1 lb. cooked beef short ribs, shredded

¼ cup roasted corn kernels

¼ cup black beans

¼ cup roughly chopped pickled red onion

¼ cup cilantro, whole leaves and stems

½ cup mashed avocado

Roasted salsa

Cotija cheese

4 corn tortillas

Instructions

1. Use a large serving platter for this appetizer.

2. At the top of the platter, arrange the shredded beef in a straight line.

3. Top the beef with corn, beans, red onion, and cilantro.

4. Use ramekins for the avocado, salsa, and cheese.

5. Warm the tortillas and place them below the deconstructed taco meat.

6. Serve by taking a tortilla and scooping a portion of taco meat with the tortilla. Use a spoon to serve from the ramekins.

PORK FRITTERS

Servings: 6
Total time: 25 minutes

Fritter Ingredients

1 lb. smoked rib meat, diced

½ onion, diced

3 jalapeños, diced (seeds removed)

½ cup shredded cheddar cheese

½ tsp. dried thyme leaves

½ tsp. garlic powder

1 cup flour

1 tsp. baking powder

Salt, to taste

1 egg

Oil, for frying

Dipping Sauce

1 tbsp. mayonnaise

1 tbsp. Hwy K Rib Sauce (page 193)

1 tsp. lemon juice

Instructions

1. Combine all Dipping Sauce ingredients in a bowl and mix well.

2. Serve immediately and refrigerate leftovers.

3. Heat oil in a deep fryer or skillet to 375°F.

4. Combine all fritter ingredients in large bowl and mix well until meat is evenly coated.

5. Make golf ball–size servings out of the fritter mix and drop them into the oil, only a few at a time.

6. Cook for 10 minutes or until golden brown.

7. Remove fried fritters and cool on a wire rack for 1 minute.

8. Serve fritters with dipping sauce.

SMOKED RIB PIZZA

Serves: 4
Total time: 1½ hours

Pizza Dough

1 cup water
1 pk. active dry yeast
1 tbsp. white sugar
2 tbsp. olive oil
4 cups all-purpose flour
1 tbsp. kosher salt
½ tsp. baking powder

Pizza Toppings

1 cup Hwy K Rib Sauce (page 193)
½ lb. cooked beef short ribs, shredded
½ lb. cooked pork spareribs (or BBR), shredded
1 lb. smoked sausage link, sliced
1 cup shredded Gouda cheese
1 cup shredded cheddar cheese
1 cup shredded mozzarella cheese
1 large fresh jalapeño, thinly sliced
1 small red onion, julienned
2 tbsp. Main Street Rib Rub (page 192)

¼ cup extra virgin olive oil, *for brushing the dough*

Instructions

1. To make the Pizza Dough, add lukewarm water (110°F) to a large bowl; add yeast, sugar, and oil. Whisk until combined.

2. Wait 15 minutes for yeast to activate (or until you see bubbles forming).

3. Add flour, salt, and baking powder and mix by hand.

4. Knead the dough for 20 minutes (do it old-school).

5. Place the dough in the bowl and cover with plastic wrap. Let the dough rest for 30 minutes.

6. Set up the cooker for direct heat at 350°F.

7. Dust a clean surface with lots of flour and start rolling out the dough. Make it somewhat round and thin; I like it to look rustic and irregular.

8. Brush olive oil on both sides of the flattened dough. To pre-bake the dough, place it in the center of the cooker and let it bake for 2 minutes (until you see grill marks). Remove from the cooker.

9. Spread ½ cup of Rib Sauce on the pizza crust. Add all the toppings evenly on the pie. Evenly apply the Rib Rub all over the pizza.

10. Place the pizza on a pizza stone and cook on the grill for 5 minutes or until the cheese is completely melted.

11. Remove the pizza from the grill and add the remaining Rib Sauce on top of the pizza.

12. Slice the pizza and serve immediately.

PULLED PORK WESTERN BURGER

Serves: 2
Total time: 5 hours

Ingredients

1 lb. ground chuck, formed into 2 patties

½ lb. cooked rib meat, pulled

6 strips of bacon, cooked

1 avocado, peeled, pitted, and sliced

2 tbsp. Honey Mustard

½ cup shredded cheddar cheese

¼ cup Hwy K Rib Sauce (page 193)

½ tbsp. Main Street Rib Rub (page 192)

4 slices of frozen garlic toast, toasted

Honey Mustard

¼ cup mayonnaise

1 tbsp. mustard

½ tbsp. Dijon mustard

1½ tbsp. honey

1 tsp. lemon juice

Fried Shallots

4 shallots, sliced into rings

Canola oil

Instructions

1. To make the Honey Mustard, combine all ingredients in a bowl and mix well.

2. Refrigerate until ready to use. You will only need 2 tablespoons of the sauce for this recipe.

3. To make the Fried Shallots, heat up canola oil in fryer to 325°F.

4. Fry the shallots for 15 minutes or until they look golden brown and crispy.

5. Set up the grill for indirect heat at 350°F.

6. Place the hamburger patties on the hot side of the cooker and cook for 10 minutes, or until you see grill marks. Cook the burgers with the lid on and the vents wide open.

7. Flip the burgers to the cool side of the grill and cook for 6 minutes. Halfway through, put the burgers in a foil pan, top with cheese, and cover with heavy-duty aluminum foil. The burgers are done when the internal temperature reaches 165°F.

8. Spread Honey Mustard on the bottom toast and top it with the burger and melted cheese, bacon, avocado, pulled pork, Rib Sauce, Rib Rub, and fried shallots. Cover with the other toast and stick it with a skewer to hold the burger together.

9. Make the other burger as above.

10. Serve immediately.

RACK 'N CHEESE

Servings: 4
Total time: 30 minutes

> Imagine that you entered a realm of the zombie apocalypse and you are being chased by the walking dead for your living flesh. Now imagine that you're running from a stampede of hungry family, friends, neighbors, and co-workers while carrying a foil pan full of Rack 'n Cheese . . .

Ingredients

2 tbsp. canola oil

2 tbsp. flour

2 cups milk

1 cup shredded cheddar cheese

½ cup shredded Monterey Jack cheese

¼ cup grated Parmesan cheese

1 lb. smoked rib meat, shredded and cooked

1 lb. elbow macaroni, cooked

¼ cup hot sauce (Valentina's, sriracha, and Frank's are my favs)

Instructions

1. To make the cheese sauce, heat the oil in a large saucepan over medium heat.

2. When the oil starts to shimmer, add the flour and mix to make the roux.

3. Slowly add in the milk (to minimize lumps) and bring it to a boil.

4. Lower the heat to low and start adding the cheese slowly, stirring until all the cheese is melted.

5. Add the pork, macaroni, and hot sauce to the cheese sauce.

6. Mix well and serve.

REDNECK "TACO"

Servings: 4
Total time: 30 minutes

Ingredients

1 lb. smoked rib meat, shredded and cooked
1 avocado, sliced
Chicharones (pork rinds), crushed
¼ cup Hwy K Rib Sauce (page 193)
½ tbsp. Main Street Rib Rub (page 192)

Sambal Slaw

1 cup green cabbage
1 cup red cabbage
¼ cup red wine vinegar
⅓ cup honey
¼ cup sambal oelek (garlic chili sauce)

Fluffy Corn Cakes

¼ cup milk
1 egg, separated
¼ cup cornmeal
¼ cup flour
½ tsp. sugar
½ tsp. baking powder
¼ tsp. kosher salt

Instructions

1. The Sambal Slaw can be made in the morning or even the day before. It should have at least an hour to chill before eating. Combine all ingredients in a bowl and mix well.

2. Refrigerate for at least 1 hour.

3. To make the Fluffy Corn Cakes, preheat a nonstick or cast-iron skillet over medium heat.

4. In a bowl, beat the milk and egg yolk together.

5. Then whisk the egg white until soft peaks are formed. (Using an electric mixer and a cold metal bowl helps here.)

6. Combine the beaten mixture with the dry ingredients and mix well. Fold the egg white in, but don't mix completely.

7. Use a ladle to scoop a serving of batter into the hot skillet. When you start to see bubbles on top of the cake, flip. Cook for another 1 or 2 minutes until golden brown on both sides. Repeat until batter is gone.

8. Put ¼ of the meat and slaw on top of one corn cake.

9. Top the "taco" with Rib Sauce, Rib Rub, avocado, and crushed pork rinds. Repeat with other corn cakes.

10. Serve immediately.

Smokers made out of 55-gallon drum barrels have been wildly popular on the competition circuit recently. The newer generations of drum barrel smokers are creative and successful on the barbecue circuit.

RIB MEAT HASH

Serves: 2
Total time: 20 minutes

Ingredients

2 tbsp. olive oil, divided

2 tbsp. unsalted butter, divided

2 cups diced and parboiled Yukon gold potatoes

¼ cup diced red bell pepper

2 cups cubed smoked pork rib meat

¼ cup golden raisins

¼ cup diced yellow onion

Seasoned salt, to taste

Garlic salt, to taste

Pepper, to taste

2 eggs

Instructions

1. In a cast-iron skillet on medium heat, add 1 tablespoon each of oil and butter.

2. Add the diced potatoes and peppers and cook until the potatoes look golden brown and delicious.

3. Add the meat, raisins, onions, seasoned salt, garlic salt, and pepper and cook for 10 minutes or until the hash starts to look crispy.

4. Top each serving with a fried egg and serve immediately.

The scenic landscape on the barbecue trail is awesome. This spot along the Meramec River is one of my favorites, and I have first dibs on it every year. . . . I'm living the dream!

RIB MEAT PARFAIT

Serves: 4
Total time: 10 minutes

Ingredients

2 cups shredded and cooked smoked pork rib meat
2 cups prepared baked beans, heated
Hwy K Rib Sauce, to taste (page 193)
Dill pickle spears

Coleslaw

1 cup shredded green cabbage
1 cup shredded red cabbage
3 tbsp. mayonnaise
¼ cup apple cider vinegar
1 tbsp. white sugar
Salt and pepper, to taste

Instructions

1. To make the coleslaw, combine all ingredients in a bowl and mix well. Refrigerate until ready to use.

2. Fill a 9 oz. cup with beans ⅓ of the way full.

3. Add a pickle spear and add the coleslaw until almost filling the cup.

4. Top off with rib meat and Rib Sauce.

5. Serve with a spoon and it's ready to eat on the go.

RIB MEAT STUFFED DOUGHNUT

Serves: 8
Total time: 30 minutes

Ingredients

8 Pillsbury Grands Flaky Layers Biscuits
Canola oil
½ lb. cooked rib meat, shredded or chopped
⅓ cup grated Swiss cheese
1 tbsp. Main Street Rib Rub (page 192)
2 tbsp. Hwy K BBQ Sauce (page 193)
1 cup granulated sugar

Instructions

1. Fill the fryer with canola oil. Preheat the deep fryer at 375°F.

2. Combine the rib meat, cheese, Rib Rub, and Rib Sauce, and mix well.

3. Open and separate the biscuits. Scoop a heaping tablespoon of rib meat and stuff it in the center of a biscuit. Stretch the biscuit dough around meat and seal it tightly with no creases. Do this 7 more times with the other biscuits.

4. Fry the stuffed dough 3 minutes or until they start to turn golden brown. Flip the doughnuts and fry for another 2 minutes, until golden brown.

5. Dip the doughnuts in sugar as they come out of the fryer and transfer to a wire rack.

6. Let the doughnuts cool for a minute and serve.

Fireside Smokers took 2nd place at the Fraternal Fires Rib Invitational. Teams were invited to compete in this special event only if they won 1st place in Ribs in previous contests within the last 12 months.

RIB SANDWICH ON STEROIDS

Serves: 2
Total time: 20 minutes

Ingredients

½ lb. smoked beef rib meat, shredded

½ lb. smoked pork rib meat, shredded

1 white onion, chopped

¼ cup Main Street Rib Rub (page 192)

½ tbsp. Hwy K Rib Sauce (page 193)

Sesame seed buns

Sweet Pickles

8 cucumbers, sliced ⅛-inch thin

¼ cup chopped red peppers

¼ cup chopped yellow onion

¼ cup apple cider vinegar

⅓ cup turbinado sugar

½ tsp. turmeric, ground

½ tsp. cloves, ground

½ tsp. celery seeds

1 tsp. mustard seeds, whole

1 tsp. Tellicherry black peppercorns, whole

⅓ cup water

Instructions

1. Make the Sweet Pickles a few days ahead. In a saucepan over medium heat, bring water and vinegar to a boil.

2. Combine the rest of the ingredients in a large mason jar and pour the hot liquid into the jar.

3. Add more water if needed and seal the jar tightly.

4. Refrigerate for at least 3 days.

5. In a skillet over medium heat, cook the beef and pork rib meat. Add a bit of sauce and rub and cook until the meat is crispy on the outside.

6. Toast the bun, then stack the meat, pickles, and onions on the bun. Repeat with second bun.

7. Top with rub and sauce.

8. Serve immediately.

SHORT RIB NACHOS

Serves: 2
Total time: 3 hours
(but start the Pinto Beans the night before)

Ingredients
Tortilla chips
1 lb. cooked beef short ribs, shredded
Oaxaca cheese
Avocado, sliced
Cilantro, chopped
Red onion, chopped

Pinto Beans
1 cup dry pinto beans
¼ cup yellow onion, diced
1 tbsp. crushed red pepper, dried
½ tbsp. Mexican oregano
½ tbsp. garlic powder
1 pk. Goya Sazón
Water, as needed

Salsa Verde
2 tomatillos
4 jalapeño peppers
2 Anaheim peppers
1 tbsp. salt
1 tbsp. garlic powder
1 tsp. cumin
½ cup diced yellow onion
¼ cup roughly chopped cilantro with stems

Instructions
1. To make the Pinto Beans, soak the beans in a bowl overnight, then strain.

2. In a large pot over low heat, add all the ingredients and stir.

3. Cover and cook for 3 hours.

4. To make the Salsa Verde, set up grill for high heat direct grilling at 600+°F.

5. Place the tomatillos and peppers on the grill and cook them until they char up and blister.

6. Put the blistered peppers in a large storage bag and seal it for 10 minutes.

7. Peel the skin off the peppers and remove the stem and seeds.

8. Put the tomatillos, peppers, salt, garlic powder, cumin, and onion in a food processor and blend until smooth. Add the cilantro in the food processor and pulse a few times to mix well.

9. Store in the refrigerator until ready to use.

10. Start building the nachos with a base layer of chips, followed by Pinto Beans, rib meat, Salsa Verde, and cheese. Top with avocado, cilantro, and red onion.

11. Serve immediately.

SHORT RIB MISSION BURRITO

Serves: 1
Total time: 30 minutes

Ingredients

Large tortilla wrap
1 lb. cooked beef short ribs, shredded
¼ cup shredded Havarti cheese
¼ cup shredded cheddar cheese
6 oz. crinkle cut french fries, cooked
1 avocado, mashed
1 Roma tomato, diced
¼ cup diced yellow onion

Chili Aioli

¼ cup mayonnaise
3 tbsp. sambal oelek (garlic chili sauce)
½ tsp. lemon juice

Bistro Sauce

¼ cup sour cream
3 tbsp. gourmet steak sauce
1 tsp. Dijon mustard

Instructions

1. To make the Chili Aioli, combine all ingredients in a bowl and mix well. Refrigerate until ready to use.

2. To make the Bistro Sauce, do the same thing—combine all ingredients in a bowl and mix well. Refrigerate until ready to use.

3. Warm up the large tortilla so that it is heated and pliable.

4. Start loading the wrap with beef, cheeses, fries, mashed avocado, ¾ of the sauces, tomato, and onions.

5. Wrap the burrito tightly.

6. In a hot skillet on medium high heat, grill the burrito until golden brown on both sides.

7. Cut the burrito in half and serve with remaining Chili Aioli and Bistro Sauce.

SHORT RIB TOSTADAS

Serves: 4
Total time: 30 minutes
(if Ancho Sauce is made ahead)

Ingredients

1 lb. cooked beef rib meat, shredded

4 tostada shells

1 cup Pinto Beans, cooked (page 195)

¼ cup Cotija cheese

2 tbsp. cilantro, chopped

Ancho Sauce

5 ancho chiles

2 whole yellow onions, chopped

6 garlic cloves, whole

1 tsp. ground cumin

1 tsp. Mexican oregano

1 tsp. kosher salt

½ cup chopped cilantro

Fried Onion Chips

Canola oil, for deep frying

½ cup flour

¼ cup cornmeal

1 cup chopped yellow onion

1 egg, beaten

Instructions

1. To make the Ancho Sauce, toast the chiles on the grill (or in a skillet on medium heat), being careful not to burn them.

2. Soak the toasted chiles in a bowl of water for 2 hours or until soft. Remove the stems and most of the seeds (keep some seeds). Reserve 2 cups of the water infused with chiles.

3. In a food processor, add all the sauce ingredients (including the water) and blend well.

4. Use immediately and store leftovers in the fridge up to 4 days.

5. To make the Fried Onion Chips, heat up oil in a deep fryer or skillet to 375°F.

6. In a bowl, combine the flour and cornmeal together and mix well.

7. Coat the onions in the beaten egg, then put them in the flour mixture.

8. Fry the coated onions for 8 minutes or until golden brown and delicious.

9. Let the onion chips cool on paper towels for 1 minute.

10. To assemble the Tostadas, put some beans on the tostada shell, followed by the meat. Top with onion chips, sauce, cheese, and cilantro.

11. Serve immediately.

SPICY PEPPER CHILAQUILES

Serves: 4
Total time: 25 minutes

Ingredients

8 jalapeño peppers, fresh
6 Anaheim peppers, fresh
4 tomatillos, husks removed
½ cup water
2 tbsp. garlic salt
2 tbsp. canola oil
¼ cup chicken stock
Tortilla chips
1 lb. shredded leftover rib meat
Oaxaca cheese
Yellow onion, julienned
Cilantro, chopped

Instructions

1. Set up grill for direct heat at 600+°F.

2. Place jalapeños, Anaheim peppers, and tomatillos on the grill and cook until they develop blisters all around.

3. Place the blistered peppers in a large storage bag and seal it. Wait 10 minutes and peel the skin off the peppers. Cut the stems and remove most of the seeds, but not all of them.

4. In a food processor, add the peppers, tomatillos, water, and garlic salt and blend until smooth.

5. In a saucepan on medium heat, add oil and strain pepper sauce into the pan. Cook for 5 minutes, then add chicken stock.

6. In a skillet on medium heat, pour in ¼ of the sauce, then add the tortilla chips. Cook until the chips are tender, about 2 minutes.

7. Serve chilaquiles with shredded pork, cheese, onion, and cilantro.

TORTA BURGER

Serves: 2
Total time: 30 minutes

Ingredients

½ lb. ground chuck
½ lb. cooked pork rib meat
2 brioche buns
¼ cup smashed avocado
2 tbsp. smashed pinto beans
¼ cup oaxaca cheese
Cilantro

Pico de Gallo

1 Roma tomato, diced
1 jalapeño, seeded and diced
2 tbsp. diced red onion
1 tbsp. chopped cilantro
2 tbsp. lemon juice

Instructions

1. To make the Pico de Gallo, combine all ingredients in a bowl. Refrigerate for 1 hour and serve.

2. Preheat the grill to high heat at 600+°F.

3. Shape the ground chuck into two patties and grill both sides until the internal temperature reaches 160°F.

4. In a skillet, cook the rib meat until the outside gets crispy.

5. On the bottom bun, spread half the avocado and beans. Put the burger on next, followed by half the rib meat.

6. Top with half of the cheese and cilantro, and ¼ cup Pico de Gallo. Repeat with other burger.

7. Serve immediately.

CHAPTER 5
PORK RIB TIP RECIPES

BLACK CANDY RIB TIPS

Serves: 4
Total time: 3 hours

Ingredients

2 lbs. pork rib tips
½ cup Main Street Rib Rub (page 192)

Black Candy Glaze

2 cups dark brown sugar
½ cup soy sauce
1 cup ginger ale
1 tbsp. red pepper flakes

Instructions

1. Set up the cooker for smoking at 250°F.

2. Apply Main Street Rib Rub on the rib tips and place them on the grate. Smoke for 1 hour.

3. Make Black Candy Glaze: In a saucepan over medium heat, combine all ingredients and reduce to simmer. After simmering for 10 minutes, cool to room temperature.

4. In a foil pan, place all rib tips in the pan. Cover rib tips tightly with aluminum foil and cook for 2 hours.

5. Cook until the pieces of pork are tender, then cut the rib tips into 1-inch cubes.

6. Brush the glaze on the meat and serve immediately.

Notes

1. Rib tips are the trimmings of pork spareribs made into St. Louis style ribs, and they're filled with bones, cartilage, and ample rib meat.

2. Use any fruitwood, hickory, or oak for smoke flavor.

St. Louis likes their barbecue ribs sweet and smoky. There is no shortage of St. Louis barbecue flavor sold locally. These barbecue rubs and sauces are from some of the best pitmasters around.

DR PEPPER RIB TIPS

Serves: 4
Total time: 4 hours

Ingredients

2 lbs. pork rib tips, cut to 2-inch portions
Main Street Rib Rub (page 192)

Foil Wrap

¼ cup Dr Pepper
1 tbsp. Main Street Rib Rub (page 192)

Dr Pepper BBQ Sauce

½ liter Dr Pepper
½ cup ketchup
1 cup brown sugar
½ cup apple cider vinegar
2 tbsp. soy sauce
½ tsp. red pepper flakes
1 tsp. chili powder
½ tsp. onion powder
½ tsp. garlic powder

Instructions

1. You can make the Dr Pepper BBQ Sauce up to 2 weeks ahead. In a saucepan over medium heat, reduce Dr Pepper for 1 hour, or until it acquires a syrup consistency.

2. Combine all the BBQ sauce ingredients in the saucepan and mix well.

3. Cook for 15 minutes, and then use an immersion blender or food processor to smooth out the sauce.

4. Let the sauce cool at room temperature until ready to serve. Store in the refrigerator for up to 2 weeks.

5. Set up the grill (or smoker) for indirect heat at 225°F. Use hickory, pecan, or any fruitwood for smoking.

6. Apply the Main Street Rib Rub evenly over the rib tips and place them on the grill.

7. Smoke for 1½ hours.

8. In a foil pan, add the rib tips and Foil Wrap ingredients. Cover the foil pan with heavy-duty aluminum foil.

9. Cook for 2 hours or until tender.

10. Uncover the foil pan and cook for 30 minutes. Baste with the Dr Pepper BBQ Sauce the last 10 minutes of cooking.

11. Serve rib tips immediately with BBQ sauce drizzled over the top.

A sweet, sticky, thick barbecue sauce is a layer of flavor to complement the unctuous taste of the rib meat. An excellent sauce should be a mixture of sweet, savory, tangy, and a little bit of spice.

PORK RIBS CONFIT

Serves: 4
Total time: 5 hours

Ingredients

2 lbs. pork sparerib tips, whole

4 lbs. manteca de cerdo (lard)

8 garlic cloves, peeled

6 sprigs fresh thyme

1 sprig rosemary

2 shallots, roughly chopped

1 bay leaf

Instructions

1. Set up the grill (or smoker) for indirect heat at 225°F. Use hickory, pecan, or any fruitwood for smoking.

2. Scoop the manteca into a deep foil pan and cover with heavy-duty aluminum foil. Place on the smoker and let the lard liquefy, about 20–30 minutes.

3. Add the rest of the ingredients to the liquefied lard and cover with foil.

4. Cook for 4 hours.

5. Take the foil pan off the cooker and let it rest for 1 hour. Place the foil pan in the fridge for at least 4 hours and up to 3 days.

6. Fire up the grill for direct heat at 600+°F.

7. Wipe off excess fat from the rib tips and set aside.

8. Sear the rib tips over high heat until a flavor crust develops.

9. Serve ribs confit immediately. This recipe is great to use for other recipes that require pulled pork.

RIB TIP CARNITAS

Serves: 4
Total time: 3½ hours

Carnitas are an authentic Mexican delicacy that is so addicting and versatile. Make it into tacos, a burrito, a sandwich . . . or add it to your salad!

Ingredients

2 lbs. pork rib tips, whole

2 navel oranges, cut in half

1 Mexican (or regular) cinnamon stick

2 bay leaves

1 medium piloncillo cone (or 1 cup brown sugar)

Lard (or canola oil)

Instructions

1. Set up the grill (or smoker) for indirect heat at 350°F.

2. In a deep foil pan, melt enough lard to submerge all the ingredients. Once the lard is liquefied, squeeze the orange juice in the melted lard, then add all the remaining ingredients (including the orange peel) to the foil pan. Cover the foil pan with heavy-duty aluminum foil.

3. Cook for 3 hours or until the pork is crispy and tender. Stir and check the rib tips every hour for doneness.

4. Remove rib tips from the foil pan and transfer them on a paper towel to absorb excess fat. Cool for 5 minutes and serve.

RIB TIPS WITH HONEY-GRAPEFRUIT GLAZE

Serves: 4
Total time: 3 hours

Ingredients

2 tbsp. unsalted butter

1 tsp. garlic, minced

¼ cup yellow onion, finely chopped

2 lbs. pork rib tips

½ cup Main Street Rib Rub (page 192)

¼ cup margarine, melted

½ cup grapefruit juice, freshly squeezed

Glaze

¼ cup grapefruit juice, freshly squeezed

½ tsp. grapefruit zest

1 cup honey

1 cup ketchup

3 tbsp. Worcestershire sauce

2 tbsp. molasses

½ tsp. Hungarian paprika

¼ tsp. ground chipotle

Kosher salt and pepper to taste

Instructions

1. Set up the cooker for smoking at 250°F.

2. Apply rub on the rib tips and place them on the grate; smoke for 1 hour.

3. Make Glaze: In a saucepan over medium heat, melt butter, then add garlic and onions. Cook until soft. Combine remaining glaze ingredients and reduce to simmer. After simmering for 10 minutes, cool to room temperature.

4. Pour juice into a foil pan and place rib tips in the pan. Cover rib tips with melted margarine. Cover tightly with aluminum foil and cook for 1½ hours.

5. Cook until the pieces of pork are tender, then cut the rib tips into 1-inch cubes.

6. Brush the Glaze on the meat and serve immediately.

TAMARIND GLAZED BABY BACK RIBS

Serves: 4
Total time: 3 hours

Ingredients

1 rack baby back ribs
¼ cup Main Street Rib Rub (page 192)

Tamarind Glaze

¼ cup tamarind paste
2 cups dark brown sugar
½ cup apple cider vinegar
1 cup ginger ale
1 tbsp. red pepper flakes

Instructions

1. Set up the grill (or smoker) for indirect heat at 225°F. Use hickory, pecan, or any fruitwood for smoking.

2. Apply the Rib Rub evenly over the baby back ribs and place them on the grill.

3. Smoke for 2 hours.

4. Wrap the ribs tightly with heavy-duty aluminum foil and place them back on the smoker.

5. Cook for 2 hours.

6. In the meantime, make the Tamarind Glaze. In a saucepan over medium heat, combine all ingredients and mix well.

7. When the paste breaks down and the glaze is smooth, the sauce is done.

8. Remove the glaze from the heat and set aside until ready to use.

9. Remove the ribs from the cooker, unwrap them, and put them back on the smoker.

10. Cook for 30 minutes. Baste the ribs with the glaze in the last 10 minutes of cooking.

11. Remove the ribs from the cooker and let them rest for 5 minutes. Cut the ribs into individual bones.

12. Serve ribs immediately drizzled liberally with Tamarind Glaze.

Bringing home the bling from the end-of-the-season Team of the Year awards banquet.

PORK COUNTRY RIBS RECIPES

CHORIZO

Serves: 4
Total time: 5 minutes

Ingredients

1 lb. country ribs, ground
½ cup canola oil
3 tbsp. white vinegar
½ tsp. ground bay leaves
1 tbsp. chili powder
½ tsp. cayenne pepper
2 tbsp. paprika
1 tsp. onion powder
1 tsp. garlic powder
½ tsp. ground cinnamon
½ tsp. ground marjoram
½ tsp. ground thyme
½ tsp. ground allspice
1 tsp. Mexican oregano
1 tsp. black pepper
1 tsp. kosher salt

Instructions

1. In a large bowl, mix all ingredients together.
2. Refrigerate overnight or up to 24 hours.
3. Cook and serve in tacos or with eggs (the traditional chorizo and eggs breakfast).

Won Reserve Grand Champion at the 2015 Rock Road BBQ Battle—this included a 9th place call in ribs.

FIREBALL COUNTRY RIBS

Serves: 2
Total time: 4 hours

Ingredients

3 lbs. country pork ribs

2 tbsp. Main Street Rib Rub (page 192)

½ cup Hwy K Rib Sauce (page 193)

Fireball Braising Sauce

½ cup Fireball Cinnamon Whiskey

¼ cup chicken stock

¼ cup white vinegar

⅓ cup brown sugar

⅓ cup ketchup

6 cloves garlic

3 bay leaves

1 tbsp. seasoned salt

1 tbsp. black pepper

Instructions

1. Set up grill (or use a smoker) for indirect heat at 225°F. Use any fruitwood such as apple, cherry, peach, etc. for smoking.

2. Apply Rib Rub evenly all over the pork. When the rub is absorbed and it looks like a glaze, the pork is ready to smoke.

3. Cook for 1½ hours in smoke.

4. In a foil pan, combine all the Fireball Braising Sauce ingredients and mix well. Place the pork in the foil and cover with heavy-duty aluminum foil.

5. Braise for 3 hours in the foil pan.

6. Set up a grill for direct heat at 600+°F.

7. Sear the country ribs until they are lightly charred. Baste with braising sauce while searing.

8. Slice pork and serve with braising sauce.

KALUA COUNTRY RIBS

Serves: 4
Total time: 5 hours

Ingredients

4 lbs. country ribs
Fresh banana leaves

Salt Compound Rub

¼ cup kosher salt
Seasoned salt, to taste
Fresh thyme, chopped

Instructions

1. First make the Salt Compound Rub. In a small bowl, combine all ingredients and mix well. Store in an airtight container or storage bag until ready to use.

2. Set up the grill (or smoker) for indirect heat at 225°F. Use hickory, pecan, or any fruitwood for smoking.

3. Apply the Salt Compound Rub evenly over the country ribs.

4. Smoke for 1½ hours.

5. Line a foil pan with banana leaves. Leave enough to cover the top.

6. Put the country ribs in the foil pan. Cover and tightly seal the foil pan with heavy-duty aluminum foil.

7. Place foil pan on the grill and smoke for another 2 hours, or until tender.

8. Remove foil cover and banana leaves and allow pork to rest for 10 minutes. Shred pork in the pan juices.

9. Serve immediately.

FILIPINO PORK SKEWERS

Serves: 4
Total time: 5 hours

Ingredients

2 lbs. country pork ribs

Filipino Marinade

⅓ cup ketchup

⅓ cup brown sugar

⅓ cup soy sauce

¼ cup sriracha sauce

¼ cup white vinegar

1 cup ginger ale

1 tbsp. red pepper flakes

1 bulb garlic, roasted and peeled

1 lime, freshly squeezed

1 tbsp. black pepper

1 tbsp. kosher salt

Instructions

1. Combine all Filipino Marinade ingredients in a large storage bag and shake to mix well.

2. Place the country ribs in the storage bag with the marinade and refrigerate for 12–36 hours.

3. Set up the grill (or smoker) for indirect heat at 225°F. Use hickory, pecan, or any fruitwood for smoking.

4. Wipe off excess marinade with paper towels and place the pork on the grill. Reserve the marinade in the storage bag.

5. Smoke for 1½ hours.

6. Pour the remaining marinade into a foil pan and place the country ribs in the pan. Cover with heavy-duty aluminum foil.

7. Braise for 3 hours, or until tender.

8. Set up the grill for direct heat at 600+°F.

9. Pierce through the pork with bamboo skewers. Sear the country ribs over high heat until a flavor crust develops.

10. Brush pork with sauce and serve skewers immediately.

PACIFIC COAST COUNTRY STYLE RIBS

First Place Ribs
Recipe by: Claudia Hermosillo

Serves: 6
Total time: 2 hours

Ingredients

3 lbs. pork country ribs
1 cup Goya Mojo Criollo Marinade
1 tbsp. garlic powder
1 tbsp. coriander
1 tsp. black pepper
2 tsp. Worcestershire sauce
½ tsp. ginger
2 tsp. teriyaki sauce
½ cup pineapple juice

BBQ Sauce

¾ of a 40-oz. bottle of Sweet Baby Ray's BBQ Sauce
2 tbsp. apple cider vinegar
⅓ cup pineapple juice
⅛ tsp. ground ginger
1 tsp. tequila

Instructions

1. Combine all ingredients except for BBQ Sauce ingredients in a plastic bag and marinate overnight.

2. Grill ribs to medium/medium-well done or about 160°F internal temperature.

3. Just before taking them off the grill, lightly slather them with BBQ Sauce on all sides and caramelize for about 1 minute on each side.

4. After taking them off grill (or just before serving), slather them again with more BBQ Sauce on top.

CHAPTER 7
RUBS, SAUCES & MORE RECIPES

All Purpose Meat Rub

1 tbsp. garlic salt

1 tbsp. seasoned salt

1 tsp. onion powder

1 tsp. paprika

1 tsp. black pepper

1. Combine all ingredients in a bowl and mix well.
2. Set aside until ready to use.

Beef Rub

¼ tsp. ground fennel

¼ tsp. celery seed

¼ tsp. chile de arbol

1 tbsp. garlic salt

1 tbsp. pepper

½ tbsp. onion powder

½ tbsp. white sugar

1 tsp. Hungarian paprika

1 tsp. Accent seasoning

1. Combine all ingredients in a bowl and mix well.
2. Set aside until ready to use.

Creole Spice Rub

½ cup paprika

1 tbsp. onion powder

1 tbsp. garlic powder

1 tbsp. cumin

½ tbsp. thyme

½ tbsp. cayenne pepper

1 tbsp. Old Bay Seasoning

1 tsp. ground allspice

1 tsp. white pepper

1 tsp. black pepper

1 tsp. kosher salt

1. Combine all ingredients in a bowl and mix well.
2. Set aside until ready to use.

Five-Spice Rub

2 tsp. Chinese five-spice seasoning

2 tbsp. paprika

2 tsp. sugar

2 tsp. crushed red pepper flakes

1 tsp. garlic powder

1 tsp. onion powder

1 tsp. kosher salt

1. Combine all ingredients in a bowl and mix well.
2. Set aside until ready to use.

Main Street Rib Rub

½ cup turbinado sugar

3 tbsp. kosher salt

1 tbsp. garlic powder

1 tbsp. onion powder

1 tbsp. chili powder

1 tbsp. Hungarian paprika

1 tbsp. black pepper

½ tsp. cayenne pepper

1. Combine all ingredients in a bowl and mix well.
2. Set aside until ready to use.

Hwy K BBQ Sauce
Makes 3¾ cups
Total time: 25 minutes

Here is an excellent rib sauce to make at home. I was inspired by a local barbecue joint that served only one sauce for all the smoked meats they offered, and I absolutely love it. With my knowledge of flavors and sensitive taste buds, I believe I came close to their recipe, but with a couple of my own tweaks . . . mustard seeds and liquid smoke. Use this as a base and feel free to add more flavors.

1½ cups ketchup
1½ cups light brown sugar
2 tbsp. tomato paste
¼ cup white vinegar
1 tbsp. Worcestershire sauce
1 tsp. mustard seeds, whole
½ tsp. garlic powder
½ tsp. onion powder
1 tsp. cayenne pepper
½ tsp. liquid smoke
½ tsp. black pepper
¼ cup water

1. Combine all ingredients in a saucepan over over medium-low heat.

2. Reduce for 30 minutes. The sauce should be thick enough to evenly coat the back of a spoon.

3. Let the sauce cool and store in the refrigerator. Store the sauce up to 2 weeks.

Ancho Sauce
5 ancho chiles
2 whole yellow onions, chopped
6 garlic cloves, whole
1 tsp. cumin, ground
1 tsp. Mexican oregano
1 tsp. kosher salt
½ cup cilantro, chopped

1. Toast the chiles on the grill (or in a skillet on medium heat), being careful not to burn them.

2. Soak the chiles in a large bowl of water for 2 hours or until soft. Remove the stems and most of the seeds (keep some seeds). Reserve 2 cups of the water infused with chiles.

3. In a food processor, add all the ingredients (including the water) and blend well.

4. Use immediately and store leftovers in the fridge up to 4 days.

Vinegar Sauce
⅓ cup Hwy K Rib Sauce
2 tbsp. yellow mustard
⅓ cup apple cider vinegar
¼ cup white vinegar
¼ cup honey
1 tbsp. black pepper
1 tbsp. red pepper flakes

1. In a saucepan over low heat, combine all ingredients and mix well.

2. Cook for 30 minutes, stirring often.

3. Turn off the heat and set aside until ready to use.

Bistro Sauce

¼ cup sour cream

3 tbsp. gourmet steak sauce

1 tsp. Dijon mustard

1. Combine all ingredients in a bowl and mix well.
2 Refrigerate until ready to use.

Chimichurri Sauce

4 cloves garlic

2 tbsp. chopped yellow onion

1 cup fresh flat-leaf parsley

1 cup fresh cilantro

¼ cup fresh oregano leaves

½ cup olive oil

1 tbsp. lime juice, freshly squeezed

2 tbsp. red wine vinegar

2 tbsp. kosher salt

2 tbsp. crushed red pepper flakes

1. In a food processor (or blender), pulse the garlic and onion until finely chopped.
2. Add the parsley, cilantro, and oregano, and pulse briefly, until finely chopped (not pureed).
3. Place the mixture in a bowl. Add the olive oil, lime juice, and vinegar, and mix well by hand.
4. Season with salt and red pepper flakes.
5. Store in the refrigerator until ready to serve.

Cheese Sauce

1 tbsp. canola oil

1 tbsp. flour

1 cup milk

½ cup cheddar cheese, finely shredded

1. Heat the oil in a saucepan over medium heat and then add the flour. Combine well.
2. Add milk slowly and stir until smooth. When the mixture starts to boil, turn the heat down to low and slowly stir in all the cheese.
3. Stir until all the cheese is melted; the sauce will thicken as it cools.
4. Refrigerate the leftovers for up to 4 days.

Honey Mustard

¼ cup mayonnaise

1 tbsp. mustard

½ tbsp. Dijon mustard

1½ tbsp. honey

1 tsp. lemon juice

1. Combine all ingredients in a bowl and mix well.
2. Refrigerate until ready to use.

Chili Aioli

¼ cup mayonnaise

3 tbsp. sambal oelek (garlic chili sauce)

½ tsp. lemon juice

1. Combine all ingredients in a bowl and mix well.
2 Refrigerate until ready to use.

Salsa Verde

2 tomatillos

4 jalapeño peppers

2 Anaheim peppers

1 tbsp. salt

1 tbsp. garlic powder

1 tsp. cumin

½ cup diced yellow onion

¼ cup roughly chopped cilantro with stems

1. Set up grill for high heat direct grilling at 600+°F.

2. Place the tomatillos and peppers on the grill and cook them until they char up and blister.

3. Put the blistered peppers in a large storage bag and seal it for 10 minutes.

4. Peel the skin off the peppers and remove the stems and seeds.

5. Put the tomatillos, peppers, salt, garlic powder, cumin, and onion in a food processor and blend until smooth. Add the cilantro in the food processor and pulse a few times to mix in well.

6. Serve immediately or store in the refrigerator.

Fried Onion Chips

1 cup roughly chopped yellow onion

1 egg, beaten

½ cup flour

¼ cup cornmeal

Oil

1. Heat up oil in a deep fryer or skillet at 375°F.

2. In a small bowl, combine the flour and cornmeal together; mix well.

3. Coat the onions in the egg, then dip them in the flour mixture.

4. Fry the coated onions for 8 minutes or until golden brown and delicious.

5. Let the onion chips cool on paper towels for 1 minute.

Pinto Beans

1 cup pinto beans, dried

¼ cup diced yellow onion

1 tbsp. crushed red pepper, dried

½ tbsp. Mexican oregano

½ tbsp. garlic powder

1 pk. Goya Sazón

Water, as needed

1. Soak the beans in a bowl overnight, then strain.

2. In a large pot over low heat, add all the ingredients and stir a few times.

3. Cover and cook for 3 hours.

Sweet Pickles

8 cucumber pickles, sliced ⅛-inch thin

¼ cup chopped red pepper

¼ cup chopped yellow onion

¼ cup apple cider vinegar

⅓ cup turbinado sugar

½ tsp. ground turmeric

½ tsp. ground cloves

½ tsp. celery seeds

1 tsp. mustard seeds, whole

1 tsp. Tellicherry black peppercorns, whole

⅓ cup water

1. In a saucepan over medium heat, heat water and vinegar. Bring to a boil.

2. Combine the rest of the ingredients in a large mason jar and pour the hot liquid into the jar.

3. Add more water if needed and seal the jar tightly.

4. Refrigerate for at least 3 days.

Sambal Slaw

1 cup shredded green cabbage

1 cup shredded red cabbage

¼ cup red wine vinegar

⅓ cup honey

¼ cup sambal oelek (garlic chili sauce)

1. Combine all ingredients in a bowl and mix well.

2. Refrigerate for 1 hour and serve.

Fried Shallots

4 shallots, sliced into rings

Canola oil

1. Heat canola oil in fryer to 325°F.

2. Fry the shallots for 15 minutes or until they look golden brown and crispy.

Sofrito

1 medium yellow onion, halved

1 red bell pepper

1 Anaheim pepper

1 head garlic, roasted

1 bunch cilantro

1 tbsp. capers

1 tsp. Mexican oregano

⅓ cup olive oil

Kosher salt and pepper, to taste

1. Set the grill to high heat at 600+°F.

2. Roast the onion and peppers. When the peppers are blistered all around, place them in a plastic storage bag and seal. Let the peppers sweat in the bag for 5 minutes, then peel the skin off.

3. Give the roasted onion and peppers a rough chop.

4. Put all ingredients (except olive oil) into a food processor and blend until smooth. Add the olive oil at the end through the top while the food processor is on.

5. Use immediately or refrigerate for 3 days.

Bleu Cheese Compound

1 stick unsalted butter, softened
3 tbsp. bleu cheese crumbles
2 cloves roasted garlic
1 tbsp. red onion, minced
½ tsp. Worcestershire sauce

1. In a bowl, combine all the compound ingredients and mix well.
2. Pour the butter compound into the center of a sheet of plastic wrap.
3. Shape the compound into a 1-inch diameter log. Wrap tightly and place it in the freezer for 30 minutes.
4. Move the butter log to the fridge until ready to use.

Coleslaw

¼ cup apple cider vinegar
⅓ cup mayonnaise
2 cloves garlic, minced
⅛ cup granulated sugar
½ head cabbage, shredded
2 cooked bacon strips, chopped
Salt and pepper, to taste

1. In bowl, whisk together apple cider vinegar, mayo, garlic, and sugar.
2. Pour dressing over cabbage, add bacon, and mix well. Add salt and pepper to taste.
3. Store in the fridge until ready to use.

Caramelized Onions

1 medium yellow onion
1 tsp. olive oil
1 tsp. Worcestershire sauce

1. In a skillet over medium-low heat, add oil and onions.
2. Cook for 15 minutes, stirring occasionally.
3. Add Worcestershire sauce and cook for another 15 minutes.

Honey Mustard Mayo Sauce

½ cup mayonnaise
¼ cup Dijon mustard
3 tbsp. honey
1 tsp. lemon juice
Kosher salt and pepper, to taste

1. Combine all ingredients in a bowl and mix well.
2. Make ahead and refrigerate until ready to use.
3. Store in the fridge for up to 4 days.

Acknowledgments

My poor vegetarian wife, Jamie, had to endure another cookbook. I acknowledge her for her patience and understanding while the sweet smoke filled our house and the meat drippings splattered on our floor and counters. The late night cooks and early morning temp checks I know were particularly annoying to her. I might as well bring my ugly drum smoker into our bedroom because that is what I smelled like in bed. Jamie, thank you again for putting up with my BBQ madness . . . but you can really only blame yourself for supporting my habit. I love you.

My BBQ team, Fireside Smokers: every competition we are pushing the boundaries of better barbecue. Our successes and failures have put us on a path of consistently being one of the best teams in the St. Louis area. I look forward to making another run at championships and trophies this upcoming season, but the journey is what keeps me coming back for more.

Lastly, I want to acknowledge my BBQ family at the St. Louis BBQ Society. Who knew such a bunch of dudes talking about smoked meats day in and day out would actually live the dream of hanging out and winning barbecue competitions? Who knew these guys could make the best BBQ rubs and sauces on the competition circuit? Ultimately, these guys are some of the best cooks and best people I have ever been around. I'm fortunate to call them my friends.

About the Author

Arthur Aguirre is the head pitmaster of Fireside Smokers BBQ Team. Starting in 2008, Arthur began smoking meats in his backyard on a charcoal Brinkman Smoker. In a couple of years, Arthur started writing recipes and contributing to various food and barbecue publications that ultimately led to the founding of his blog *Major League Grilling*.

In 2010, Arthur entered his first barbecue competition and placed 4th overall. This led Arthur to pursue barbecue glory, with better smokers, on the competition circuit under the name Major League Grilling. After years of competing in various sanctioning bodies such as the Kansas City Barbecue Society and the St. Louis BBQ Society and now competing as Fireside Smokers, Arthur has achieved a great amount of success.

As Fireside Smokers BBQ Team, Arthur and his teammates have won multiple Grand Championships, Reserve Grand Championships, Top 10 calls in all four main protein categories: chicken, ribs, pork, and brisket. In addition, a Top 10 finish—in the St. Louis BBQ Society Team of the Year points chase—cements his status as one of the best pitmasters in the region.

Arthur is living the dream of cooking award-winning barbecue; however, even more rewarding are the relationships that are built through his journey. Some of his best friendships have been established because of barbecue. It never amazes him when barbecue is a topic of discussion—whether in a grocery store, ball game, work, etc.—how many folks want to become your friend.

METRIC AND IMPERIAL CONVERSIONS

(These conversions are rounded for convenience)

Ingredient	Cups/Tablespoons/Teaspoons	Ounces	Grams/Milliliters
Oil	1 cup=16 tablespoons	7.5 ounces	209 grams
Cheese, shredded	1 cup	4 ounces	110 grams
Flour, all-purpose	1 cup/1 tablespoon	4.5 ounces/0.3 ounces	125 grams/8 grams
Fruit, dried	1 cup	4 ounces	120 grams
Fruits or veggies, chopped	1 cup	5 to 7 ounces	145 to 200 grams
Fruits or veggies, puréed	1 cup	8.5 ounces	245 grams
Honey or maple syrup	1 tablespoon	.75 ounces	20 grams
Liquids: milks, water, vinegar, or juice	1 cup	8 fluid ounces	240 milliliters
Salt	1 teaspoon	0.2 ounces	6 grams
Spices: cinnamon, cloves, ginger, or nutmeg (ground)	1 teaspoon	0.2 ounces	5 milliliters

Fahrenheit	Celcius	Gas Mark
225°	110°	¼
250°	120°	½
275°	140°	1
300°	150°	2
325°	160°	3
350°	180°	4
375°	190°	5
400°	200°	6
425°	220°	7
450°	230°	8

INDEX